GETTING MORE HEAT
FROM YOUR FIREPLACE

By Paul Bortz

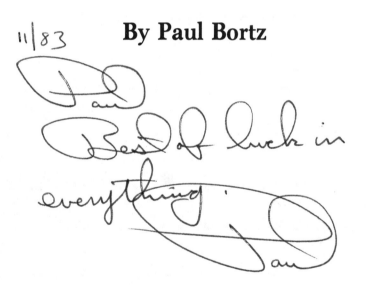

11/83

Best of luck in everything.

GARDEN WAY ✿ PUBLISHING
Charlotte, Vermont 05445

*This book is dedicated to my four daughters whose
continued presence is both a joy and reminder of the
obligations that we all have to one another and our society.*

Catherine, Ellen, Alice and Clara

Copyright 1982 by Garden Way, Inc.

Printed in the United States

Cover design by Trezzo/Braren Studio

Illustrations by Robert Vogel

Library of Congress Cataloging in Publication Data

Bortz, Paul, 1941-
  Getting more heat from your fireplace.
  Includes index.
  1. Fireplaces. I. Title.
TH7425.B67   697'.1   81-13389
ISBN 0-88266-254-6   AACR2

Contents

The family fireplace is often the center of a beautiful living room, but seldom is it an efficient source of home heat.

CHAPTER 1

Fireplace Efficiency: Past and Present

Warmth and security, hospitality and togetherness . . . these are just a few of the feelings kindled by the flames of a fireplace . . . a popular source of home heat. There are an estimated 25 million fireplaces in the United States, and the number is increasing. Two out of three new homes are built with conventional, masonry fireplaces. Unfortunately, these are usually inefficient, often grossly inefficient. If you have one, you may have discovered how little heat it produces.

Like most of us, you still want the romance and beauty of the open fire *and* every bit of warmth possible from the wood, coal or other solid fuel you burn. That's often difficult to achieve. Fires demand oxygen and they consume it voraciously. A typical, three-log fire in a masonry fireplace takes four times more air out of a room than the amount needed to keep a fire going. That's *expensive, warm* room air — going right up the flue.

This kind of performance bothers me. I'm sure it bothers you.

But, there are ways to get more heat from your fireplace — everything from building better fires to installing new, more efficient appliances: stoves, inserts and tubular grates with blowers. I'm going to discuss these and other products. And, for those who want more information, there's a catalog of manufacturers at the back of the book with product specifications, descriptions and photos.

When you review these products, keep in mind that they will perform differently, depending upon conditions at your home. The room size and temperature, the design of your house, the shape and height of the flue, the wind velocity and direction — these and other factors affect fireplace appliance performance. Before installing a new appliance or accessory, examine your fireplace and flue carefully (Chapter 9). If you doubt the safety of your chimney, seek professional assistance. (For more information on selecting appliances, see Chapter 5.)

FIREPLACE EFFICIENCY

Although there are many new heat-saving devices available today, efforts to get more heat out of a fireplace have been going on for more than 400 years. The outcry following the 1973 Arab oil boycott wasn't the first time the public became aware of energy shortages. Fuel shortages have occurred in centuries past and men like Louis Savot, Prince Rupert, Benjamin Franklin and Count Rumford were among the pioneers in the development of more efficient fireplaces. All were seeking ways to generate more heat from less fuel.

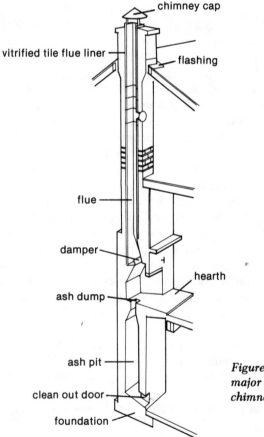

Figure 1-1. Here are the major parts of a typical chimney and fireplace.

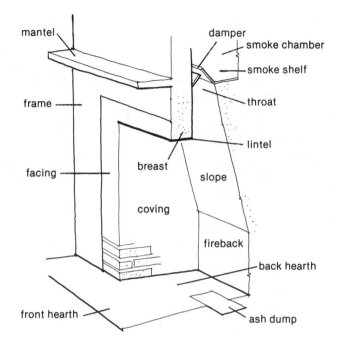

Figure 1-2. These are the details of a masonry fireplace.

The Fireplace and Chimney

To better understand the achievements of these men, let's take a quick look at the parts of a typical masonry fireplace and chimney (Figure 1-1).

The fireplace *foundation*, often made of concrete, supports a significant weight — each cubic foot of brick weighs up to 150 pounds. Above the foundation is the *ash pit*. Coals and ashes are raked into a metal opening, called the *ash dump*, which is located in the floor of the *hearth*. Ashes may be dumped as often as necessary. The ashes drop into the ash pit below where they remain until removed. (By the way, the potash in wood ash is good for gardens, lawns and trees.) At the base of the ash pit is the ash *cleanout door*.

In many homes, the chimney has a dual function. When enclosing two flues, it serves as an outlet for smoke and gases from both the fireplace and furnace. In such cases, the furnace (not shown) attaches with a furnace exhaust pipe to the furnace flue which runs up the chimney next to the fireplace flue.

For details of the fireplace level, see Figure 1-2. The fireplace *front hearth* is made of stone or brick and extends far enough into the room to protect the floor from hot coals and sparks. At the base of the firebox and contiguous with the front hearth is the *back hearth*, where the fires are built. Usually, the back of a fireplace has two parts: 1) the *fireback*, against which a fire might rest; and 2) the upper portion called the *slope* of the fireback. The slope reflects heat and flames toward the room. On either side of the back are the *sides* or *covings*. The *lintel* supports the top of the fireplace opening. Also shown are the fireplace *mantel, frame* and *facing.*

Just inside and above the lintel is the *breast.* Above and behind the breast is the *throat,* an opening 3 to 4 inches wide. Over the throat is the *damper* which may be used to close off the throat or adjusted to control the rate of combustion in the fireplace. Usually made of cast iron for longer life, this device may be opened by turning a damper handle or by reaching into the firebox and pushing a lever attached to the damper.

A *smoke shelf* is at the base of the *smoke chamber.* This chamber helps prevent cold air from coming down the chimney and entering the room. Cold air that enters the chamber hits the smoke shelf, mixes with smoke and rises back up the chimney.

The chimney has, or should have, a protective *flue liner* made of clay tiles. The tiles are held together with a heat-resistant cement. Often a "dead" air space is left between the flue liner and the outside brick to enhance insulation. If your chimney is unlined, flue tiles or stainless steel pipe can be lowered down the chimney.

At the top of the flue is the *chimney cap* or cover. When installed, the cap helps prevent wildlife, foreign objects, rain and snow from entering the flue. Preventing the mixture of water and smoke by-products is important; this mixture causes a corrosive chemical reaction which slowly "eats" away at tile, mortar, brick, smokepipe and other chimney material.

Yesterday's Efficiency

Fireplaces, as we know them today, emerged in Europe about 1200 A.D. (See chronology, page 6.) These were enclosed fireplaces with a hood over the hearth and a chimney to exhaust smoke to the outside. One of the first recorded efforts to get more heat from fireplaces occurred about 200 years later. This effort resulted in the use of cast-iron firebacks which reflected more heat into a room by reducing the depth of the fireplace. Firebacks also slowed mortar and brick deterioration in an age when special fireplace brick and refractory mortars were unknown.

In the late 16th and early 17th centuries the cost of wood increased and soft coal replaced wood as the heating and cooking fuel. Special coal grates for fireplaces were developed to enable easy ignition and combustion of this

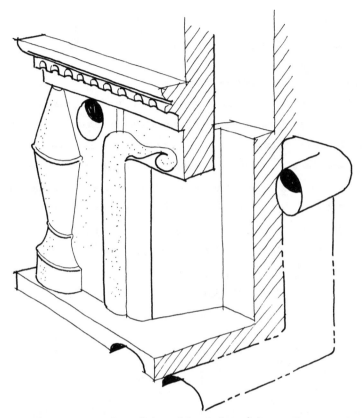

Figure 1-3. This is an artist's rendition of Louis Savot's innovative, seventeenth century fireplace. Air entered at the base, and, after warming, exited beneath the mantel and circulated out into the room.

fuel. Coal represented a significant, new, home-heating alternative. Using coal meant more heat from the fireplace at less cost.

More heat at less cost was also the aim of these well known innovators:

Louis Savot. About 1620, a Frenchman named Louis Savot experimented with fireplaces and improved their efficiency by circulating room air through a fireplace "jacket" (Figure 1–3). In effect, the jacket created a fireplace within a fireplace. Cooler room air entered the jacket bottom, circulated around and up the back and then out the front just below the mantel. Savot's design preceded, by about 200 years, what is now known as a heatalator fireplace, a unit that improves efficiency by using the same kind of air circulation as that incorporated in the seventeenth century French design.

TRACING FIREPLACE EFFICIENCY

circa 1200	Conventional fireplaces in use
1400 to 1500	Cast iron firebacks appear
circa 1600	Louis Savot experiments with circulating fireplaces
1600s	Coal, supported by grates, used in home fireplaces
circa 1600	Germans use cast iron doors to cover fireplace
late 1600s	Prince Rupert develops fireplace with baffles
1713	Gauger publishes work on reflecting fireplace sides and backs
1741	Benjamin Franklin invents Pennsylvanian Fireplace
circa 1750	Count Rumford designs efficient fireplaces
1758	Franklin writes on fireplace dampers
circa 1780	Blast furnace developed for making cast iron
1812	Coal grate added to Pennsylvanian Fireplace
1835	Bessemer steel process enables mass-produced stoves
1836	Isaac Orr patents airtight stove
1850s	Fireplace dampers in use
circa 1850	Automatic thermostat for stoves
1870	Fireplace inserts, stoves
1930s	Factory-built fireplaces
1940s	Tempered glass doors
1970	Tube grates with blowers
1975	Modern fireplace inserts
1975	Central fireplace furnaces

About the same time, German craftsmen discovered that cast-iron doors used to close off a fireplace at night would prevent the escape of warm room air up the chimney. Although prevalent in Germany, this practice was not widely accepted throughout Europe in the seventeenth century. Today glass doors and night covers are common, and the German doors probably are their predecessors.

Count Rumford. In 1713, a Frenchman named Gauger wrote a significant paper emphasizing the importance of designing fireplace backs and sides with slopes to reflect more heat into a room. Count Rumford, who re-

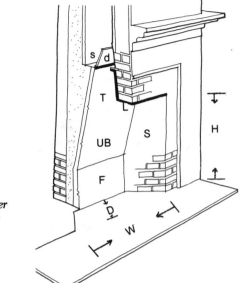

Figure 1-4. Details of the Rumford design include: height (H), width (W) and depth (D). Also, the fireback (F), throat (T), sides (S), upper back (UB), lintel (L), damper (d) and smokeshelf (s).

ceived British knighthood for his many scientific inventions, saw the merit in Gauger's work and incorporated it into a new fireplace design that became known as the Rumford fireplace (Figure 1-4). With its narrow throat, sloping back and broad, reflective surfaces, Rumford's fireplace was dramatically more efficient than the designs that preceded it.

Rumford's design included many principles of fireplace construction that are still valid today:* the fireplace opening should be as high as it is wide; the depth should be one third of the opening width; and the fireback should be as wide as the fireplace depth. The throat opening, Rumford said, should be about one tenth of the fireplace opening and have a width of about 4 inches. Both sides should be angled to the back, and the back should be about 13 inches wide. The lower back should be straight, while the upper portion should slope to meet the 4-inch wide damper opening. The throat should be toward the front of the firebox and at least 8 inches above the lintel; the smoke shelf should be at least 10 inches deep.

Benjamin Franklin. In the 1740s Benjamin Franklin, concerned about a possible wood shortage and alarmed by the prospect of a nation dependent upon imported fuel, introduced the Pennsylvanian Fireplace. His invention looks much like a stove and is sometimes referred to as the Pennsylvanian Stove or Franklin's Fireplace Stove. Although the Pennsylvanian Fireplace was complex and probably difficult to install, it incorporated the best

---

*These principles could be used when designing an efficient fireplace for a new home or when redesigning an existing fireplace.

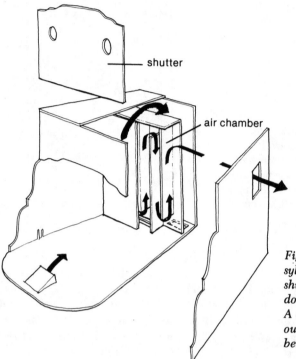

shutter

air chamber

Figure 1-5. The Pennsylvanian Fireplace. A shutter could be slipped down over the opening. A chamber warmed outside air brought in beneath the fireplace.

of the design features that preceded it and clearly influenced the design of fireplace appliances that followed (Figure 1-5).

Franklin knew the meaning of efficiency long before it became a popular concern. He was distressed by the way ordinary masonry fireplaces performed. "In common chimneys," he wrote, "the strongest heat from the fire, which is upwards, goes directly up the chimney and is lost . . . in these sorts of fireplaces . . . five sixths [83 percent] . . . of the heat . . . is wasted. . . ."*

Franklin's figures are not far from those discovered in the 1970s and 1980s by trained specialists working in scientific testing laboratories. Furthermore, Franklin predicted with uncanny accuracy the necessity for developing more efficient fireplace appliances to remove the danger that the nation might become dependent upon foreign fuel (in those days, coal). He said his invention would help save firewood and allow owners to warm themselves at a "moderate rate, without being oblig'd to fetch their fuel over the Atlantick. . . ."*

What were the innovative features of this inventor's remarkable stove? The 14 different pieces were sealed tightly together with mortar cement. The Pennsylvanian used fresh, outside air to aid combustion. A damper controlled the air flow. Further combustion control was achieved with a large, sliding front plate or "shutter." The plate could be slipped up or down when the fire was banked for the night.

Not only did the shutter improve control and prevent the escape of warm room air when the stove fire waned, it also allowed those seated nearby to view the flames, a pleasure uppermost in the minds of many home-heating appliance buyers today. Other important features of the Pennsylvanian Fireplace included:

- A baffle system that required smoke and gases to travel about 5 feet. This meant more time for heat to be extracted from the escaping gases and smoke, and thus more heat for the room.

- A chamber for the outside air fitted with heat transfer fins. Again, this innovation allowed for the retention and transfer of more heat into a room and reduced heat loss up the chimney.

Franklin was convinced that the Pennsylvanian used much less wood than conventional fireplaces. "People who have us'd the Fire-Place differ much in their accounts of the wood saved by theirs. Some say five sixths, others three fourths, and others much less . . . I suppose, taking a number of families together, that two-thirds, or half the wood at least is saved. My common room I know, is made twice as warm as it used to be, with a quarter of the wood I formerly consum'd there."*

Other Steps Toward Efficiency

While Franklin's fireplace stoves are seldom used today, his improved design influenced the wood stove industry for 250 years. Even after the introduction of his stove, the famous Philadelphian continued to suggest design improvements for fireplaces. In 1758, for example, he described in writing a fireplace damper to be placed in the throats of chimneys. He speculated, accurately, that such a device would slow the loss of room air.

Despite the advantages of dampers, which now appear obvious, not until the mid 1800s were dampers commonly added to new flues. About 1812, a coal grate was added to Franklin's fireplace stove, giving it a multi-fuel capability.

In 1836, an American named Isaac Orr patented an "air-tight" stove. The term *airtight* was subsequently used to describe those stoves having tight joints and controlled drafts. Most of today's airtight stoves are more efficient than those that are not.

---

*Jared Sparks, ed., *The Works of Benjamin Franklin* (Chicago: Townsend MacCoun, 1882).

The mass production of these stoves and dampers and grates accelerated with the development of the blast furnace used for manufacturing cast iron and the invention of the Bessemer process (1835) for making steel. But with the discovery of "cheap" oil and natural gas, oil- and gas-fired furnaces became the primary source of home heat. Although most suburban and rural homes had fireplaces, they were there for aesthetic reasons, not to generate heat.

20th Century Developments

With the Depression in the 1930s, conservation and energy efficiency again resurfaced as important concerns. In this period, factory-built or heatalator-type fireplaces were introduced. These units extracted and circulated more heat from the fire and flue gases than did conventional fireplaces.

During World War II, conservation was again of concern. This time fireplaces were modified with tempered-glass doors. When closed at night, these doors prevented significant heat loss up the chimney. The post-war period, however, brought massive economic expansion and energy consumption.

Fireplace Efficiency Today

Not until the early 1970s and the Arab oil boycott, were major, new efforts made to improve fireplace efficiency. These efforts included the design and mass production of special grates and blowers, more efficient airtight stoves and fireplace inserts.

Many of these products have been tested by various laboratories and assigned efficiency ratings. Efficiency ratings tell how much useful heat can be gained from a home heating appliance in relation to the amount of fuel consumed. Ratings will vary from unit to unit because of different design features and quality of construction.

Efficiency figures are sometimes misleading, however, because the way you operate a unit in your home may differ from the way it was operated when tested. The efficiency of a home-heating appliance is affected by many variables, including the weather, air infiltration in the house and the size and design of the chimney flue.

Nonetheless, while it is difficult to assign exact efficiency figures to general categories of fireplace appliances, enough studies have been done to establish approximate efficiency ranges. (Keep in mind, too, that there are ways to improve fireplace efficiency without purchasing an expensive new appliance. These will be discussed in Chapters 2 and 3.)

To get a general notion of the efficiency ranges possible with various accessories and heating appliances, see Figure 1–6. In general, fireplace heating appliances are more efficient if they are airtight, if they have baffles or some means for greater internal circulation of gases, and if they have fans or blowers to force heated air forward into a room.

ordinary straight-back fireplace

manufactured fireplace (heatalator)

fireplace with reflective shield

glass doors

manufactured fireplace with blower

free-standing fireplace

radiant grate

radiant grate and shield

natural convection tube grate

tube grate with shield,

tube grate with blower

tube grate with blower and shield

forced tube grate with glass doors

fireplace stove

zero-clearance fireplace

fireplace furnace

fireplace insert

solid-fuel furnace

free-standing stove

Sources: Auburn University, University of New Mexico
Lawrence Berkeley Laboratory

Figure 1-6. These are approximate efficiency ranges for various home-heating devices, appliances and fireplaces.

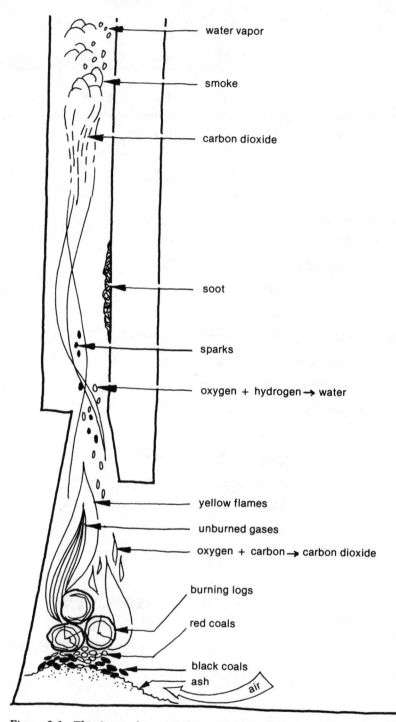

Figure 2-1. This figure shows combustion occurring in a fireplace. By-products include ash, soot, smoke and water.

CHAPTER 2

Building Better Fires

The art of building a fire, much like the art of building a good fireplace, has often suffered from neglect. In recent years, though, more and more homeowners have experimented with their fireplaces, trying to generate as much heat as possible. Some homeowners are burning coal. Many are paying attention to lessons passed on by their grandparents. By their example, these older people demonstrate the fine art of fire building. In this chapter I've summarized the best of these oldtime practices. First, to better understand your fireplace, let's digress a bit and talk briefly about combustion (Figure 2-1).

UNDERSTANDING FIREPLACE FIRES

Wood, the most common fireplace fuel, is comprised of carbon, hydrogen and oxygen. These elements represent stored potential energy that is released through combustion. In addition to the solid fuel and oxygen, temperatures must be high enough (about 600 to 700°F.) to achieve ignition and continuous combustion. When combustion occurs, a chemical reaction causes the carbon to mix with the oxygen, forming carbon dioxide; and the hydrogen combines with the oxygen to form water. When combustion is incomplete, further by-products are released, mainly tar and creosote. Other indications of incomplete combustion are blue flames, dense, dark smoke and a residue of large coals or ashes after the fire has gone out.

Forms of Heat

During combustion, energy stored in the fireplace logs is released as heat in three forms (Figure 2-2). *Conducted* heat passes through an object or surface from the hotter to colder area. For example, a spoon placed in hot coffee becomes hot quickly, but the end of the spoon at the bottom of the cup is always hotter than at the end away from the liquid. In this case, heat has been conducted or transferred from the coffee to the spoon and, to a lesser degree, to the handle. In a fireplace, heat often moves from the flames, air, smoke and masonry up the chimney material.

Heat is also transferred through *convection*. This occurs as air is heated and circulates away from its source, i.e., the fireplace fire and masonry. In a typical freplace, naturally-circulating room air, usually rising from a low point to a high point, pushes some heat into the room; most rises up the chimney flue.

Radiation involves the emission of infrared rays from the fire. When there are neither glass doors nor a fireplace screen to obstruct the rays, they heat whatever is in line with the fire. Radiated heat warms any nearby surface or material. This can be sensed by sitting near a fire; the body surfaces in line with the fire will be warm, while the side of your body away from the fire will be much cooler.

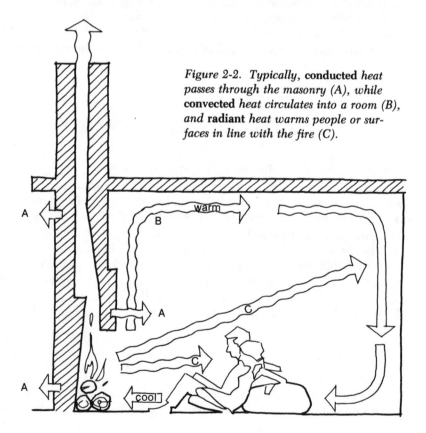

*Figure 2-2. Typically, **conducted** heat passes through the masonry (A), while **convected** heat circulates into a room (B), and **radiant** heat warms people or surfaces in line with the fire (C).*

EIGHT WAYS TO BUILD BETTER FIRES

One of the simplest ways to increase the heat output from your fireplace is to build a better fire. Here are eight methods that will help you get more heat from a conventional masonry fireplace:

Figure 2-3. If possible, allow ashes to build up below fire.

1. **Build Your Fire on a Good Ash Base.** A base of ashes about 2 or 3 inches deep acts as an insulator that not only reduces heat absorption by the fireplace hearth, but reflects heat back up into the fire. This, in turn, keeps fire temperatures high enough to enhance combustion. It's best to build your fire directly on the ash base.

If you are using andirons, let the ashes build up to within 1 to 2 inches of the fire base so less air will get beneath the flaming logs (Figure 2–3). This will inhibit heat loss up the chimney, and enable better combustion control. A low-to-medium fire, not a roaring or smoldering fire, produces sustained, even heat.

Figure 2-4. The available heat from green firewood is about 15 percent less than that for air dry firewood.

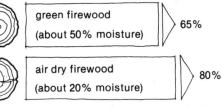

green firewood (about 50% moisture) 65%

air dry firewood (about 20% moisture) 80%

total available heat (by volume) 100%

2. **Use Dry, Spark-Free Wood.** Dry wood with a moisture content of less than 20 percent generates more heat than does wet, green wood (Figure 2–4). See Table 2–1 for a comparison of various fuel woods. To gauge the dryness of your wood, listen to the fire. There should be no "hissing" sounds soon after the fire has been ignited. A good practice is to cut your firewood a

TABLE 2-1. RATINGS FOR FIREWOOD*

	Relative amount of heat	Easy to burn	Easy to split	Does it have heavy smoke?	Does it pop or throw sparks?	General rating and remarks
Hardwood Trees						
Ash, red oak, white oak, beech, birch, hickory, hard maple (sugar, rock, black), dogwood	High	Yes	Yes	No	No	Excellent.
Soft maple, cherry (red), walnut	Medium	Yes	Yes	No	No	Good.
Elm, sycamore, gum	Medium	Medium	No	Medium	No	Fair – contains too much water when green.
Aspen, basswood, cottonwood, yellow poplar	Low	Yes	Yes	Medium	No	Fair – but good for kindling.
Softwood Trees						
Southern yellow pine, Douglas fir	High	Yes	Yes	Yes	No	Good – but smokey.
Cypress, redwood..........	Medium	Medium	Yes	Medium	No	Fair.
White cedar, eastern red cedar .	Medium	Yes	Yes	Medium	Yes	Good.
Eastern white pine, balsam fir, hemlock, red pine..........	Low	Medium	Yes	Medium	No	Fair.
Tamarack, larch..........	Medium	Yes	Yes	Medium	Yes	Fair.
Spruce..........	Low	Yes	Yes	Medium	Yes	Poor.

*Adapted from: "Firewood for your Fireplace." U.S. Forest Service, U.S.D.A. Leaflet No. 559.

year in advance and to keep at least one week's supply of wood inside your home during the heating season. Wood left outside absorbs moisture like a sponge, unless it's covered.

Also, it's a good idea to select a dry wood that is less likely to pop or crackle. Crackling woods include white or red cedars, tamarack, larch and spruce. Although these woods make good kindling, they spark so much that a screen is usually required. And that's a serious disadvantage. A fireplace screen significantly reduces the flow of heat from your fireplace into the living room. (For more discussion of screens, see page 27.)

3. Use Softwoods for Kindling and Hardwoods for Logs. Whenever possible, use the softwoods for kindling. Softwoods, especially pine, produce hot coals quickly. And these coals raise temperatures around the logs for fast-starting and more complete combustion.

For the main fire, use hardwoods. Because they are denser, hardwoods generate up to twice the heat per log of softwoods. For example, a cord of white pine, cedar, balsam, fir or spruce produces 14.5 million Btus while a cord of hard sugar maple produces 27 million Btus. And this means, with hardwoods, that cutting, handling, stacking and storing are greatly reduced.

4. Use Long Logs. Cut logs to sizes that fill the width of your fireplace. Many people build fires with logs only one-half to two-thirds as long as the fireplace opening. Longer logs offer greater surface area to reflect heat into your living room. Furthermore, long logs are convenient; by using them, you will need to reload the fire less frequently.

5. Arrange Logs to Retain and Reflect Heat. Many homeowners unintentionally lay logs in their fireplaces in ways that inhibit, rather than enhance, the movement of heat into the room. For example, some place a log near the back, kindling in the middle and a log in the front. They then add more kindling on top of these two base logs, and then add a top log. This is sometimes called a triangular arrangement (Figure 2–5). It's easy to build

Figure 2-5. A conventional, three-log fire.

and ignites quickly, but it seldom reflects heat forward. Much of the heat is lost up the chimney.

A better method is to arrange the logs against the back of your fireplace so they reflect heat out into the room (Figure 2–6). First, whenever possible, place a large green back log, approximately 12 to 15 inches in diameter, against the fireplace back wall. This will reflect heat back into the fire, as well as into the room, and slow the rush of heat up the chimney. Then arrange your kindling and three logs in front of the back log. Place the logs close enough so they keep each other hot, but far enough away so that oxygen can mix about the logs for combustion. After several fires, the green log dries out; simply add it to your fire and replace it with another green log. These logs also reduce the size of the firebox, and thereby move the fireplace heat closer to you.

Figure 2-6. To reflect heat forward, use this log arrangement.

6. **Build a "Firebox" Fire**. Another way to arrange your fireplace logs has been devised by J.M. Dullin of Libertyville, Illinois. He places two logs on either side of the kindling with their ends facing forward. Then he adds logs at the back of the fireplace that reflect heat toward the living area (Figure 2–7). The effect is similar to that created by a back log. I've tried this type of fireplace fire with good results. I prefer to lay the fire directly on an ashbed, rather than on a grate or andirons.

7. **Strive for an Even, Red-Hot Bed of Coals**. A red-hot bed of coals, about 1½ to 2 inches thick, provides good, steady, even heat. (For an indication of coal-bed temperatures see Table 2–2). To create red-hot coals, tend the fire as carefully and as continually as possible, poking and prodding when necessary. Add a log every half hour or so, as needed, instead of

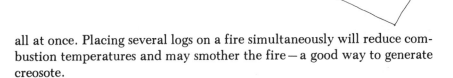

Figure 2-7. This arrangement also reflects heat forward. Replace back logs as necessary to keep the fire going.

all at once. Placing several logs on a fire simultaneously will reduce combustion temperatures and may smother the fire — a good way to generate creosote.

TABLE 2-2. THE APPROXIMATE COLOR OF GLOWING HOT, SOLID OBJECTS*

	Temperature	
Appearance	*°F*	*°C*
No emission detectable	Less than 885	Less than 475
Dark red	885–1200	475–650
Dark red to cherry red	1200–1380	650–750
Cherry red to bright cherry red	1380–1500	750–815
Bright cherry red to orange	1500–1650	815–900
Orange to yellow	1650–2000	900–1090
Yellow to light yellow	2000–2400	1090–1315
Light yellow to white	2400–2800	1315–1540
Brighter white	Higher than 2800	Higher than 1540

*Adapted from D. Rhodes, *Kilns* (Philadelphia: Chilton Book Co. 1968).

TABLE 2-3. FUEL COMPARISONS

	Approx. gross Btu per lb.	Ease of starting	Special grate needed	Visual characteristics of fire	Pounds to equal one gallon of oil or 140 cubic feet of natural gas. (140,000 Btu)
Wood: Maple/Oak	9,000	Easy – difficult	No	Excellent flames and varied colors	24 lbs.
Wood: White Pine	4,500	Very easy	No	Excellent flames and varied colors	40 lbs.
Coal: Anthracite	15,000	Very difficult	Yes	Very low orange flame	13 lbs.
Coal: Bituminous	14,000	Difficult	Yes	Red, orange or blue flames	12–13 lbs.
Coal: Lignite Briquettes	10,000	Easy	Yes	Red, orange or blue flames	17 lbs.
Peat Bricks	6–8,000	Very easy	Yes	Low flame	20 lbs.
Pelletized Organic Fuel	9,600	Difficult	Yes	Low to medium flame (most brands)	15 lbs.
Compressed Fuel Logs	8,000	Difficult	Yes	Medium flame	16 lbs.

8. **Observe Knowledgeable Old Timers and Others Who Know Fireplaces.** This may seem unscientific, but I've learned a lot by watching older people who have been building efficient fires for years. Don't ask them how they do it, just observe and learn.

One tip I learned: if there are unburned pieces of wood or partially burned pieces, be sure to add them to your next fire. I know one person who sifts his ashes through a screen to be sure none of these pieces is overlooked. This charcoal-type wood can generate a lot of heat.

COAL AND OTHER SOLID FUELS

Pound for pound, coal can be a better, more convenient fuel for your fireplace than wood. Some coals give off up to 40 percent more heat per pound than dry hardwood (Table 2–3). And coal provides a long, steady fire once established. Coal is also more manageable — no more cutting, splitting and stacking. Processed solid fuels, such as pellets and briquettes, have similar advantages as well.

Coal has disadvantages, too. It does not have the bright, cheerful blaze of wood. Coal gives off carbon monoxide gas, and this means that *adequate ventilation is essential.* Difficulty igniting, back puffing and poor combustion are among the indications that a coal fire is inadequately ventilated. Solutions include opening the damper farther or opening a window a crack. If problems persist, ask a professional chimney sweep or mason to examine your chimney.

Burning Coal

Coal can not be burned in a fireplace without kindling; it is too difficult to ignite. The best way to proceed is to add a few handfuls of coal to an already-established wood fire. Don't add too much coal at once because you might smother the fire. You may need a special coal grate to keep the fuel elevated for air circulation (Figure 2–8). This is especially important for hard, anthracite coal. Sufficient air circulation beneath the fuel is needed for successful ignition and combustion.

There are some other characteristics of coal you should be aware of. Most American coals have a high ash content, and this leads to the formation of *clinkers* or pieces of burnt coal fused together. Although clinkers are less likely to form in a fireplace than in a coal stove, you might encounter them occasionally. Because clinkers will eventually choke off the air supply, they must be broken up with a poker. Coal by-products, such as soot, must be re-moved. If mixed with moisture, sulphuric acid might form, and this can damage metal, mortar and brick. (See Chapter 9 on fireplace and chimney maintenance.)

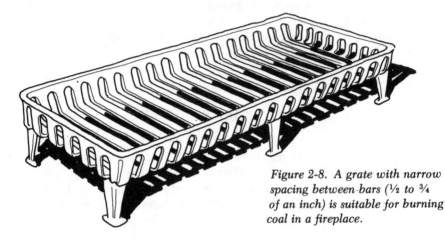

Figure 2-8. A grate with narrow spacing between bars (½ to ¾ of an inch) is suitable for burning coal in a fireplace.

Selecting the Right Coal

A good coal dealer will help you select the best coal for your fireplace or heating appliance. Often, your choice is limited to the type available or the type specified by the manufacturer. Do *not* burn coal in an appliance in-tended for woodburning only. When selecting a coal look for:

- Uniformity and suitability of size (grate and heating appliance manu-facturers often recommend the best size for their grates)
- A low ash content (less than 10 percent)
- A low sulphur content (less than 2 percent when possible, otherwise less than 3 percent)

Most coals are sold by the ton, so you'll need a bin that's easily accessible, both for the fire tender and for the dealer making deliveries.

Here are the most widely used coals and methods for burning them in fireplaces.

Anthracite. Also known as *hard coal*, anthracite is preferable to soft, bituminous coal because it contains fewer volatile gases and gives off less of an odor. Yet, it is a steady, slow-burning coal, and its sulphur content is apt to be low. Compared to bituminous, it is relatively clean. Igniting anthracite and maintaining a fire, however, are often difficult.

Usually, a good, hot bed of coals from a wood fire is necessary to ignite anthracite. Be sure the damper is open before ignition. Add a few coals initially, then more as the fire continues. As with wood fires, optimum efficiency is achieved with steady, medium coal fires with the damper near, but never *in*, the closed position.

Bituminous. Bituminous coal works well in a fireplace. It ignites and burns relatively easily. Extra caution must be taken with bituminous, however. Good ventilation is a must, to ensure that unburnt volatile gases exhaust up the flue.

Cannel. Like anthracite, cannel coal burns cleanly and has little odor. Its availability may be somewhat limited because the coal is mined in only a small number of geographic areas. It gives off volatiles that burn with a brilliant orange flame; it also produces sparks so be sure a fireplace screen is used. Cannel coal comes in large chunks and is usually sold in 50-pound bags or boxes because of its limited supply.

Coal briquettes. Brick-shaped coal briquettes are made of processed and cleaned, low-grade coal by-products. They have a low sulphur content and burn cleanly. Typically, briquettes produce about 10,000 Btus per pound. They can be used in most masonry fireplaces and stoves with brick liners. Because they are imported to the United States, briquettes tend to be a relatively expensive fuel.

Processed Solid Fuels

Since World War II, when fuel was scarce, researchers in the United States have been trying to produce clean fuels from reconstituted organic products, including garbage. Europe already relies heavily on these processed solid fuels. In Great Britain, for example, 20 percent of all home-heating fuel comes from specially processed organic compounds. Increased use of these fuels can be expected in the United States as energy costs continue to climb. Here's a brief look at some of the processed fuels now available:

Compressed wood logs. Compressed wood by-products, such as sawdust, chips and bark, can be shaped into artificial logs suitable for fireplaces. Most are sold in packs of three logs or in boxes. Each pound of "logs" contains about 8,500 Btus, or an amount approximately equivalent to hardwood. Compressed logs are clean burning, with little smoke or ash, and they produce less creosote than wood. They burn slowly, lasting between four and six hours. They are expensive and some are suitable only for fireplaces and *not* heating appliances.

Coal logs. Coal logs are a combination of compressed wood chips and bituminous coal. These logs produce about 10,000 Btus per pound, but they may give off a stronger odor than is generally acceptable to most fireplace owners.

New products. One future fuel is a mix of garbage, sludge and low-grade coal, compressed into briquettes. Another potential fuel, peat, is abundant in the United States but not widely used. In Ireland, Finland, and the Soviet Union, peat is burned extensively. Its strong odor might be alterable through special processing. Compressed into briquettes, peat might become a major home-heating fuel.

CHAPTER 3

Low-Cost Ways to Improve Fireplace Efficiency

After building a good fire in your fireplace, you want it to provide as much heat as possible to you, to your living room and to your home. Some of the ways I've tried do not *add* heat, but do reduce heat loss; others add heat without the expense of a new fireplace appliance or heating unit. These ways include: eliminating conventional grates and making better use of andirons; limiting use of the traditional "heat-stopping" fireplace screen; using glass doors effectively; and installing reflective firebacks and heat-saving night covers.

Do Away With Grates

The conventional fireplace grate was developed in Europe more than 300 years ago, primarily to facilitate the burning of coal. A grate elevated the coal, permitting good air circulation around the fuel, and aided combustion. Grates were often used in the United States in the latter half of the nineteenth century and first quarter of the twentieth. When coal use subsequently declined, the grate remained because it made starting wood fires easy.

Although a grate may help you start a fire by allowing air to circulate freely below the kindling, a conventional grate allows *too much* air into the fire after it is going. And combustion proceeds too rapidly. The solution? Eliminate the grate and replace it with andirons or — even better — build your fire directly on a bed of ashes.

One authority, Frank Rowsome, thinks grates are useless and a detriment to effective fire building. "Bunching lengths of wood together in an iron cage (grate) has more convenience than charm," he writes, "the conve-

nience being achieved not so much by making skilled fire tending unneces-
sary as by making it impossible."*

What About Andirons?

While preferable to grates, andirons are another anachronism. In an-
cient times, they were used to support meat cooked over a fire with a spit.
The two "end irons" (andirons), driven into the ground, supported the
"spit." As cook stoves were developed in the 1800s, the fireplace was slowly
abandoned as a place for cooking, but the andirons stayed.

Many people consider a fireplace incomplete without andirons, and
there are some advantages to these attractive accessories. They are preferable to grates because they allow sufficient, but not excessive, air circulation, and they protect your hearth and floor from rolling logs. Andirons
also allow partially-burnt logs to fall down into the coals; this enhances
continuous combustion. Grates, on the other hand, keep logs and kindling
elevated.

If you do use andirons, space them about 12 to 15 inches apart. Under-
neath, let a bed of ashes build within 1 or 2 inches of the andirons, then lay
newspaper, kindling and logs on the andirons.

A fire can be built most effectively, as I've suggested, if it's placed directly on ashes and andirons or grates are removed. Arrange logs carefully
so they don't roll forward. A split log placed in the front of the fireplace
should retain the others. Or, you could place a 4-inch-high steel bar across
the front of the fireplace opening to prevent logs from rolling forward (Figure 3–1). Bricks can serve the same purpose.

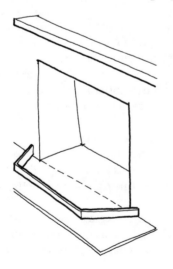

Figure 3-1. A steel bar, placed across the fireplace opening, will help retain ashes, coals and logs in the fireplace.

Use a Fireplace Screen Properly

The fireplace screen has an obvious and important function: to prevent "live" sparks from flying out into the room. At the same time, the screen decreases the amount of heat entering the room. It's been called a "heat-robbing abomination."*

A simple test demonstrates the screen's impact. Light a fire and, after it's under way, place the screen in front. Hold your hand 6 inches from the outside of the screen. Wait 30 seconds. Leave your hand in place and remove the screen with your other hand. Wait 30 seconds again; feel the increased heat. One study found that at least 30 percent less heat reaches a room when a fireplace screen is in place.**

The best thing to do with a fireplace screen is to remove it. If the fire can't be watched continually, though, this is obviously unwise. So, the next best step is to use a screen that is high enough to retain sparks but open on the top to permit upward and forward movement of heat. Place the screen as far away from the fireplace face as is safely possible (see Figure 3–2).

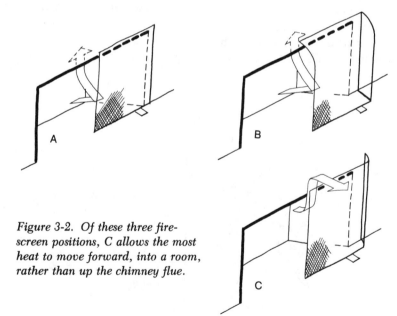

Figure 3-2. Of these three fire-screen positions, C allows the most heat to move forward, into a room, rather than up the chimney flue.

*Frank Rowsome, *The Bright and Glowing Place* (Brattleboro, Vt.: Stephen Greene Press, 1975).

**Robert D. Busch et al, "Analysis of Heat-Saving Retrofit Devices For Fireplaces" (New Mexico Energy Institute, University of New Mexico, 1979).

The Fireplace Damper

I know of no other fireplace mechanism that's more important than the damper (Figure 3–3). It enables control, and combustion control is essential to the efficient operation of a fireplace. Lacking a well-maintained, properly-functioning damper, a fireplace is a lot less efficient than it should be. Adjusting a damper requires attention, but it is not difficult if your damper control handle is outside the fireplace, near the lintel. If your damper lever is inside the firebox, you may need a poker or some other tool to adjust it.

Inspect the damper periodically, perhaps several times a year, to ensure that it fits tightly when closed. There should be absolutely no air holes or spaces when the damper is in the closed position. If necessary, seal around the damper plate with refractory cement applied with a putty knife. Check also that there are no cracks in the cast iron and that the adjustment mechanism is in good working order.

If your damper leaks or needs replacing, consider installing a chimney-top damper mechanism. This damper, made of die-cast aluminum seals the top of the chimney tightly (Figure 3–4). It is designed to provide protection from weather and to retain chimney heat between fires. When a chimney is warm, draft improves and the chances of creosote condensation diminish. The damper is adjustable from within the home at the level of the fireplace face.

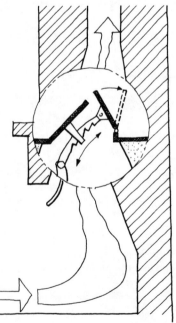

Figure 3-3. A typical, notched-bar fireplace damper. The damper may be opened or closed by adjusting the position of the bar. It is important that the damper fit tightly.

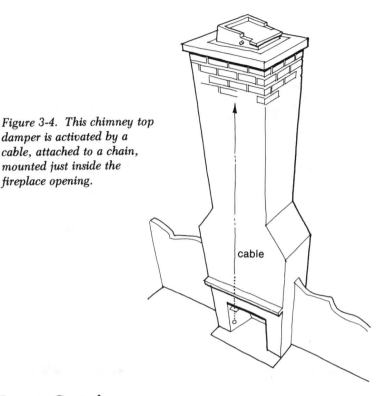

Figure 3-4. This chimney top damper is activated by a cable, attached to a chain, mounted just inside the fireplace opening.

cable

Damper Control

The damper is designed to minimize the escape of air and heat from a fireplace. During a fire, it is usually necessary to adjust the damper repeatedly. Wind, outside temperatures, infiltration through door or window cracks and flue temperatures (which influence the flue's ability to draw) are among the factors likely to change and thereby necessitate damper adjustments. Figure 3–5 illustrates a series of suggested damper positions during the six stages of a typical fireplace fire.

A damper should, of course, always be closed when the fireplace isn't in use and nearly closed when you have a good fire going. To adjust your damper for minimum heat loss, close it to a point where a small amount of smoke from the fire spills into the room, then open it just a touch. In this position, the damper will slow the combustion rate, while reducing the amount of room air and heat that is drawn up the chimney.

With a damper in a near-closed position, the potential for creosote buildup increases. Check the condition of the chimney flue at least once every week. If creosote buildup persists, burn smaller, hotter fires and open the damper more.

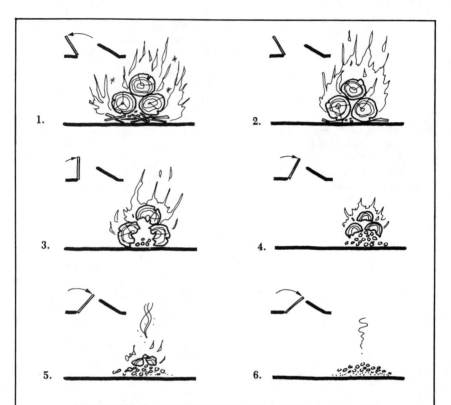

FIGURE 3-5. THE STAGES OF A TYPICAL FIRE

A typical, three-log fireplace fire, ignited and left unattended, passes through these six stages:

Stage 1. Ignition: Fire lit; spark, oxygen and fuel combine to begin combustion; smoke usually heavy.

Stage 2. New fire: Burning of most kindling complete; initial ignition of logs; large flames; high temperatures; medium to heavy smoke.

Stage 3. Mature fire: Most outside log surfaces burning; flames low and steady; smoke light.

Stage 4. Waning fire: Flames diminishing; logs burnt through; hot coals; light smoke and gases.

Stage 5. Hot-coal fire: Flames extinguished; very few large pieces of wood; glowing bed of coals; little smoke.

Stage 6. Smoldering fire: Few hot coals; ash buildup; little or no heat; a few live coals remain for reignition; no smoke.

Firebacks

For more than 500 years, the cast-iron fireback has been used as an attractive and practical fireplace piece. The fireback's original purpose was to protect mortar and bricks from deterioration; that was before mortar designed to resist high temperatures was generally available. But, the fireback serves another important function: it reflects radiant heat from the fireplace into the living area.

When handling a fireback, use caution and follow the manufacturer's instructions for installation. These cast-iron pieces can be bulky and often weigh 40 to 50 pounds. Typically, they measure about 15 to 20 inches wide and about 20 inches tall. Firebacks are available with decorative, colonial patterns.

There are at least three ways to install a fireback in a fireplace: 1) mounted against a back wall of the fireplace with anchors and steel screw hooks; 2) leaning against a back wall; and 3) leaning against a back wall and elevated on bricks. In all three positions, the fireback helps reflect heat forward. The first installation (Figure 3–6A) is likely to provide the most reflection and is intended for fireplaces with straight or curved backs. The second method (Figure 3–6B) is the simplest. And the third (Figure 3–6C) has a specific purpose: reducing the chance of smoke flowing into a room.

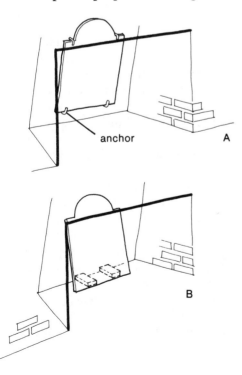

anchor   A

Figure 3-6 (A, B, C). Here are three possible ways to install a fireback in a masonry fireplace.

B

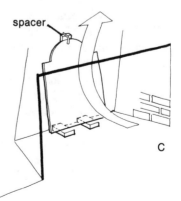

spacer

C

To mount a fireback using the first method, begin by locating the fireback in the position shown in Figure 3–6A. Then mark appropriate points for the anchors. The anchor holes should be drilled into the mortar, using a masonry bit. The bit size depends on the anchor size. Follow the manufacturer's recommendation. Once the holes have been drilled, insert the anchors. These are like plugs that have threaded openings into which screw hooks can be inserted. Pennsylvania Firebacks of Philadelphia, Pennsylvania, recommends durable steel anchors with a ¼-inch thread size and 2½-inch-long steel screw hooks, also with a ¼-inch thread (Figure 3–7). Once the anchors are in, screw in the hooks that hold the fireback in place.

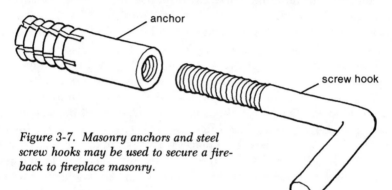

Figure 3-7. Masonry anchors and steel screw hooks may be used to secure a fireback to fireplace masonry.

The second installation is probably not as effective as the first. That's because a fireback leaning against a fireplace back wall reflects some heat upward, rather than down into the fire or out into a room. Nonetheless, a fireback resting against a back wall at only a slight angle also reflects heat forward while protecting the masonry.

The third installation involves mounting the fireback on bricks to reduce interior smoking (Figure 3–6C). When the fireback is set in this elevated position, a draft is created and air tends to circulate toward the back of the firebox, carrying smoke with it.

Firebacks can also serve another function — to shorten deep fireboxes. This can be accomplished by mounting the fireback on support brackets or "legs" and placing it forward, away from the back wall. In this position, the fireplace fire is closer to the room so less heat goes up the chimney and more heat is reflected forward. Experiment to determine the best position for the fireback in your own fireplace. Place it as far forward as possible, but not so far that it causes smoke to spill into the room. (Firebacks probably would *not* be useful for this purpose in fireplaces with a depth of less than 14 inches and a width of less than 30 inches.)

To cure a new fireback, build several small, successive fires against it.

This gradual process of expansion and contraction will cure the iron for future use under normal conditions. Rapid expansion of uncured cast iron caused by excessive initial heating can cause your fireback to crack. Do not expose a fireback to high-temperature coal fires. Excessive, sustained heating can warp cast iron. Do not expose a fireback to water; this can crack, warp or rust it.

Banking a Fire

Ideally, a fire should be out before you retire for the night or leave your home. Aside from the obvious safety reasons, there's a practical reason as well. Once the fire is out, you can close the damper to prevent warm room air from escaping up the chimney. If you want to extinguish a fire as quickly as possible (without resorting to water or extinguishers), stand the logs on end at the back of the fireplace and spread out the bed of ashes.

If you want to retain a fire overnight, follow these steps:

First, build up a good base of hot coals, then cover them with a ½- to 1-inch layer of ash. Do not smother the coals or pack ash on them; the aim is to provide enough air to keep them "alive".

Second, reduce the air flow by closing the damper most of the way. To reduce the air flow further, cover the fireplace face with a night cover.

Next morning, uncover the face, open the damper, remove the ashes from the coals, rake the coals into a pile, and add kindling and small logs. Your fire will reignite. Unfortunately, overnight fires provide little, if any, heat, but reignition the following morning is easy.

Night Covers

If you already own glass doors, you have an efficient way to reduce the flow of heat out of your fireplace at night or when a fire is waning. If you haven't, a night cover fabricated from steel, millboard or some other noncombustible material is another option. Night covers can also be purchased, complete and ready to install. Some night covers, either purchased or fabricated, have legs that enable you to stand the cover up against the face. Another type of night cover is like a roll-up shade, secured to brackets installed along the top of the fireplace opening. This flexible cover is rolled down over the fireplace face when the fire is waning or out.

How to make a night cover. The materials for a home-fabricated, folding night cover are a piece of sheet metal (24 gauge), ¼-inch noncombustible material (asbestos millboard); a pair of non-mortise hinges, small bolts,

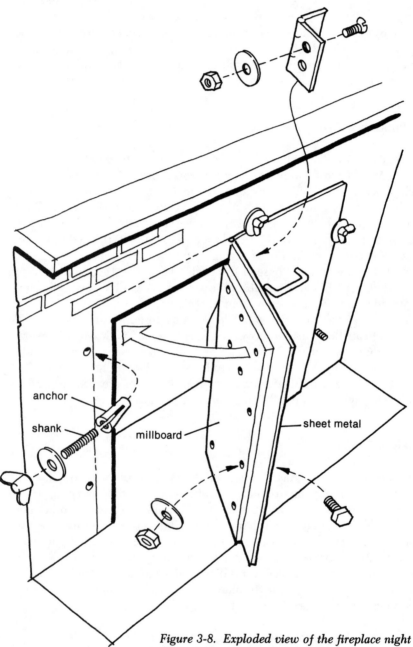

anchor

shank

millboard

sheet metal

Figure 3-8. Exploded view of the fireplace night cover, secured to the facing with anchors, threaded shanks, washers and nuts.

washers, threaded shanks, and nuts; a pair of handles; and masonry anchors to secure the cover to the fireplace opening.

This night cover may be fabricated using these tools: a circular power saw, a drill and twist bits, two adjustable wrenches, four C-clamps or spring clamps and a pen or pencil for marking.

Follow these steps and refer to Figure 3–8 when making your cover:

1. Measure the width and height of your fireplace opening.

2. Add 4 inches to the width and 2 inches to the height. Divide the width in half to give the sizes for the two sheet-metal sections. Have the sheet metal cut to size.

3. Start with the actual dimensions of the fireplace opening again. Cut two sections of the asbestos millboard to the height and half the width of the fireplace opening.

   To cut asbestos boards, clamp in succession the edges to be sawed between pieces of plywood. This will prevent the sheets from cracking and breaking while being cut. Wear a respirator mask to avoid breathing dangerous asbestos dust, and vacuum it up promptly when finished.

4. Clamp a section of asbestos to a section of sheet metal. Place the clamped sections on a flat surface, asbestos side up, with pieces of scrap wood under each clamped side. Drill out corner holes (drilling through both asbestos and metal), and bolt the four corners together. Remove the clamps. Now, drill out two or three bolt holes, spaced evenly between the corners. Secure with bolts, washers and nuts in these holes.

   Repeat this process with the next section.

5. Place the two combined sections together on a flat surface, the metal side up. Put the two hinges in place (evenly spaced) and mark for hinge holes. Remove the hinges. Place a wooden block under each area to be drilled and drill out the hinge holes. Bolt hinges on.

6. Drill out the handle holes and mount the handles.

7. Place the night cover up against the fireplace opening. Mark four points where you plan to attach the night cover to the masonry. Drill out the holes at these points with a masonry bit.

   Put anchors in place and screw in the threaded shanks. Washers and nuts attached to these shanks will hold the cover in place.

8. If you wish to provide a tighter seal between the fireplace and cover, an even, 2-inch wide surface strip may be secured around the fireplace

opening with cement or some other suitable adhesive material. If you don't want the strip to show when the night cover is removed, it could be cemented onto the cover itself.

After spending an evening in front of your fire, you can use the night cover to reduce the amount of air available to the fire and thereby slow down combustion until the fire goes out. But, most important, the night cover will cut off the flow of warm air in your house up the flue — until the damper can be closed.

Be sure to leave the damper open until you are absolutely certain the fire is dead. As the fire slowly smothers, smoke and noxious gases will be produced. Once the fire is out, the danger of these gases no longer exists, and the damper can be closed.

CHAPTER 4

Glass Doors, Tube Grates and Combination Units

If you're looking for ways to get more heat from your fireplace (or reduce heat losses) while retaining the pleasure of an open fire, there are three possibilities in the mid-price range. These are more expensive than the accessories described in Chapter 3, but less expensive than the full-sized fireplace appliances described in Chapters 5 through 8. The mid-price options include new glass doors, tube grates and what I call "combination" units. This last appliance combines in a single unit the best features of glass doors and tubular grates. These combination units are also known as fireplace heat exchangers.

GLASS DOORS

Glass doors don't add heat to your living room; they reduce heat loss. From a practical standpoint, they have the same purpose as a night cover. Glass doors should be closed only during the waning stages of a fire when little heat is being produced and the potential for heat loss up the chimney is great. Never burn with both the glass doors and the integral sliding screen shut; even the screen, if shut, will impede the transfer of heat into the room. A free-standing screen on the hearth about a foot from the fire contains sparks and allows for more radiant heat than a sliding screen.

Selecting Glass Doors

When selecting glass doors for your fireplace, you can choose from various designs, finishes and materials. Many different-sized, glass-door units are available. One company, Portland Willamette, of Oregon, sells 66 standard sizes and many custom sizes as well.

Almost all glass-door units have these major components: a frame, tempered glass doors and adjustable air intake slots. Special brackets or anchor bolts hold the door frame to the fireplace. Insulation on the back of the frame helps seal it to the fireplace masonry. Usually, an integral spark screen is included with the frame.

Most units weigh about 60 pounds. In general, the heavier the unit and the more expensive it is, the more likely the doors will be of good quality. When selecting a glass, I prefer tempered Pyrex or a comparable product because these can stand the kind of thermal shock that might be produced in a fireplace. Look for a glass-door unit with at least a one-year warranty on the frame, and make your purchase from a reputable, well-established dealer.

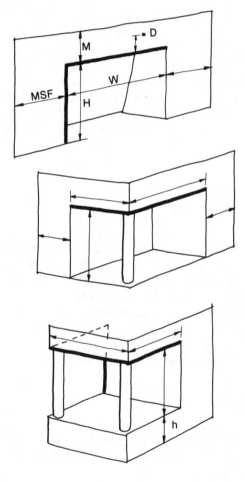

Figure 4-1. When ordering glass doors (or fireplace screens), furnish an accurate sketch and these measurements to the manufacturer or dealer: height (H), width (W), distance to damper (D) and mantel (M), width of masonry side facing (MSF) and hearth height (h).

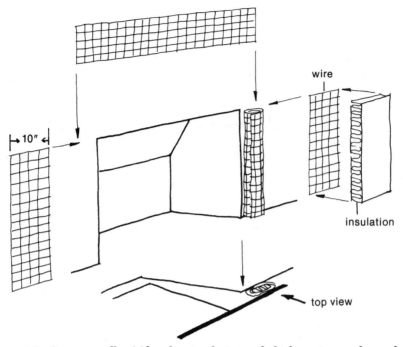

Figure 4-2. Compact rolls of fiberglass insulation and chicken wire can be used to fill gaps behind door frames or flanges.

Know your fireplace dimensions. Before ordering glass from a manufacturer or dealer, you will need to know your fireplace dimensions. Include these with your order. Figure 4–1 illustrates typically required data. When taking these measurements, pay particular attention to the location of the damper handle. Avoid glass-door units that will interfere with the operation of the damper.

Protruding bricks, stone fireplace faces or other uneven surfaces or implements also must be noted and accommodations made for them. A stone face is not impossible to fit, but spaces between the stone and the door frame should be filled. You can use thick fiberglass insulation between the back of the frame and the face. For large gaps, you can make a roll of chicken wire and insulation and insert this where needed (Figure 4–2). Cut long, 10-inch wide strips of chicken wire and matching strips of fiberglass insulation (without foil backing). Roll these together to form a compact, 3- or 4-inch diameter roll. Mold the roll into the stone gaps and secure it with anchor bolts. Then compress the door frame against the face of the fireplace. These procedures are also suitable for eliminating gaps behind the frames or flanges of inserts and other heating appliances.

Glass Door Installation

In most cases, installing glass doors in a fireplace takes about two hours, sometimes less. No special tools or equipment are needed. An electric drill, masonry bits and hand tools may be required, if bolts or screws are used to secure the frame to the fireplace masonry. Often the frame is secured with adjustable brackets.

In the fall, stove stores or fireside shops sometimes offer worthwhile, free clinics on glass door installation. For the most part, you'll probably have to rely upon the manufacturer's installation instructions which usually follow this kind of a sequence:

1. Assemble the doors.

2. Mark the fireplace face for anchor bolts (if used).

3. Secure the door frame to the fireplace with either screws, bolts or brackets.

4. Open and close doors and screen to ensure proper operation.

Building a Fire

If you decide to install glass doors, it's a good idea, for safety reasons, to build your fires on a grate. Although it does not improve efficiency, a grate is needed to retain the logs and keep them from rolling forward into the glass. A grate is preferable to andirons because hot andirons, if close, might break the glass. Place the grate at least 3 inches from the doors, so logs can touch neither the glass nor the door frame. Once again, when a grate is used, it's a good idea to accumulate a base of ashes to within 1 or 2 inches of the bottom of the grate. The ashes will reduce excessive air circulation while retaining the warmth of the fire near its base.

Maintenance

To keep your glass doors in good condition, check them periodically for possible defects. Pay special attention to the condition of moving parts. Check hinges and latches carefully. Also, check connections between the door frame and fireplace (screws, bolts or brackets) for security.

Closed glass doors that deprive a fire of air can also increase creosote buildups due to slower rates of combustion and cooler fires. So, check the flue at least once a week for creosote. (For more details on fireplace and flue maintenance, see Chapter 9.)

At times, the glass doors may appear sooty and dark. It's important to clean the doors for practical as well as aesthetic reasons. Soot and creosote can impair the ability of tempered glass to withstand temperature changes. When cleaning the glass, use only a solution recommended by the manufacturer; ordinary household cleaners may be abrasive enough to etch the glass. Clean the doors *only* when they are at room temperature or cooler, never when hot. Cool liquid striking hot glass may shatter the glass because of the temperature extremes. Also, check the glass for cracks. If replacement is necessary, use only a quality tempered glass (such as Pyrex) that can withstand high temperatures.

TUBE GRATES

As mentioned earlier, most conventional fireplace grates do not improve efficiency and should be removed. On the other hand, there are more effective new grates of tubular design that help carry heat into a room. Most are a series of tubes or some kind of piping designed to transfer heated air. The C-shaped tubes take in cool air at the base of the unit and then, after the air is warmed by passing near the base, back and top of the fire, it is convected from the tubes back into the room (Figure 4–3).

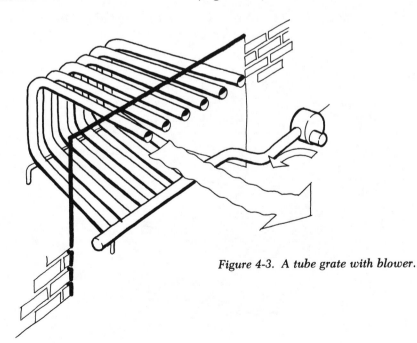

Figure 4-3. A tube grate with blower.

The heat output of these units is improved with the addition of a blower. Sometimes a blower may be added to the series of tubes; in other cases, the unit may come with an integral blower. In either case, the units work about the same. A reflective plate welded to the back of the unit further improves the heat transfer capability of this appliance.

There are at least 20 manufacturers of tube grates. Be careful that you select a model that is durable; pick one that carries at least a two-year warranty and is made of stainless steel or is "double walled." The reason durability is important is that some tube grates have been known to "burn out," actually deteriorate under the heat of a normal fireplace fire.

Another item that sometimes burns out is the electric-powered blower. Make sure the blower you purchase has a variable-speed motor with a noise level that's acceptable to you. Dealers don't mind if you test the blower in the store.

With or without a blower, the top pipes of the tubular grate should extend *beyond* the fireplace face. This ensures that warm air comes out into the room instead of recycling inside the fireplace or through the lower tubes of the grate. Some manufacturers include extenders with the grate; others sell them at additional cost.

Flat-tube Fireplace Grates

Another model is a horizontal, flat-tube fireplace grate (Figure 4–4). Characteristically, these units "pick up" and circulate mostly bottom fire-

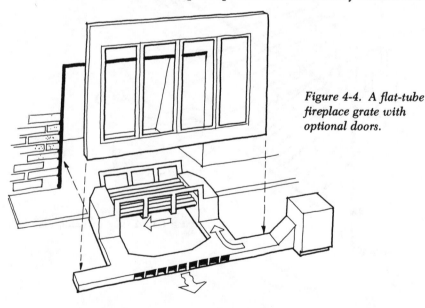

Figure 4-4. A flat-tube fireplace grate with optional doors.

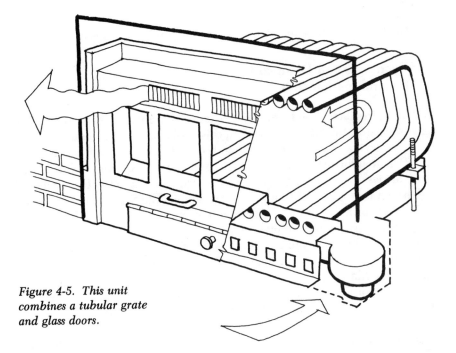

Figure 4-5. This unit combines a tubular grate and glass doors.

place heat and some back heat. These units do not have piping that extends over the top of the fire; therefore, they do not circulate heat rising from the flames.

COMBINATION UNITS

Yet another possibility for your fireplace is a combination unit: a fireplace appliance that combines in one unit the best features of tubular blower grates and glass doors (Figure 4–5). With this combination, more combustion control — and efficiency — is possible than with either glass doors or grates alone. In some cases, glass doors and grates may be purchased separately, then "combined" to form a complete unit. Or you can buy a unit with both doors and grates already assembled as one unit. Usually the latter alternative is more expensive and slightly more difficult to install, but combustion control is better.

You can reasonably expect to double or even triple your fireplace efficiency with a combination unit. Blower grates alone increase efficiency. However, the rate of combustion is more difficult to control with just grates because air rushes through the fireplace opening and over the grate, cooling the fire with excess air before continuing up the chimney.

Advantages and Disadvantages Of Combination Units

These fireplace appliances transfer more heat into the living area than any other unit talked about so far in this book. They offer about the same combustion control as a freestanding, non-airtight stove, but are only half as efficient as an airtight vented into a fireplace flue. Usually, combination units are less expensive than a fireplace insert stove and easier to install than a freestanding stove. With a combination unit, the fire remains in view.

During normal operation, excessive creosote is not a problem because the combustion rate in a combination unit is high enough to produce hot flue gases. But, when a combination unit is sealed tightly, and the intake of combustion air is severely reduced with the damper nearly shut, creosote may accumulate. In any case, inspect the unit and flue frequently.

Another disadvantage: there may be limitations on the installation of these units. Ask the manufacturer if installation is possible in fabricated metal fireplaces. Often it is not. Cleaning and flue inspection also may be difficult because combination units are usually anchored to the fireplace. On the other hand, most fireplace inserts and freestanding stoves are even more difficult to install or remove.

Assembly and Installation

Detailed assembly and installation instructions are provided by most manufacturers. Because combination units are available in many different designs, it's impossible to provide precise instructions here. However, you can expect that assembly of these units will take two to three hours; installation might require another hour. *Before you start to assemble any fireplace appliance, check that all parts are included in the shipping carton.*

Combination units are secured to the fireplace various ways. On some, the back of the glass door frame is sealed to the fireplace face and cracks are filled with fiberglass insulation. The seal should prevent air leaks; if there are leaks, warm room air will escape when the fireplace is unused or the fire waning. Many models are not only sealed and secured at the frame, they are also fastened to the hearth with anchor bolts.

Operation

For safe operation of tube grates and combination units, read the manu-

A combination unit offers more combustion control than either a simple tube grate or glass doors used alone. (Courtesy Aquappliances, Inc.)

facturer's instructions carefully. When adding wood to your fire, always turn the blower off to avoid damage from ashes that might get sucked into the unit. Some grates and combination units have thermostats that increase the blower speed automatically as the temperature of the fire increases. It is important to have the blower on when a fire is well under way for the best heat transfer and the least damage to the grates.

Another way to help extend the life of a grate is to leave enough space between the lower tubes and the ash base so hot coals can fall through easily. Avoid an ash base that's high enough to suspend the coals about the grate. With a few inches of space, the chances of grate burn out are reduced. Also, a few inches is the optimum distance for combustion—not far enough to cause excessive air circulation and close enough to reflect heat back into the fire.

There's disagreement in the industry about whether the glass doors of a combination unit should remain open or closed during a fire. Most manufacturers recommend keeping the glass doors closed. This differs from my earlier recommendation to leave *conventional* fireplace glass doors open except during the fire's waning stages. With the glass doors of a combination unit closed and the blower on, the unit captures heat and circulates it forward to a room. Even though the closed doors impede the forward movement of radiant heat, they also prevent the escape of warm room air up the chimney. Therefore, many manufacturers believe, the most efficient way to operate a combination unit is with the doors closed.

I go along with this recommendation, but I also think it's worthwhile to try to evaluate how your unit performs. It may be that during the initial, high-flame stages of a fire, you will get more heat from a combination unit with the glass doors open. Also, with the doors open, there's probably less chance that creosote will form in a chimney.

Finally, for long-term, efficient operation of a combination unit, or of any fireplace appliance, take notes on the unit's performance. How long does a fire burn using specific types and amounts of wood? How is it affected by various damper or air inlet settings? How do your heating bills change? These are items you should note and compare, to assess a unit's performance. The important thing is not to become fixed upon a specific method of operation. Instead, experiment to determine what works best in your home.

Maintenance

Like any fireplace appliance, a little periodic care will ensure a longer life for tube grates or combination units. Clean the grate exterior with steel wool to remove soot and creosote. Do this any time there's an accumulation of 1/6 of an inch or more. If the tubes are not clean, the transfer of heat from the unit will be impeded.

If you can obtain a refrigerator condenser-coil brush, it's a good implement to clean the inside of the tubes. Sometimes, though, this is impossible because the tubes are inaccessible. At the end of the wood burning season, clean the unit thoroughly. Remove it from the fireplace and store, or protect it from moisture that might pass down the chimney.

Also, clean the glass doors as necessary (see pp. 40–41).

CHAPTER 5

Selecting a Heating Appliance For Your Fireplace

So far, I've discussed several low-cost ways to get more heat from your fireplace. For the most part, these methods require few changes to your fireplace and little adaptation. Now I'd like to talk about selecting more substantial, more expensive and more efficient appliances. These include fireplace inserts, freestanding fireplace stoves and conventional stoves adaptable to fireplaces (Figure 5–1).

Often, these terms are confused or used interchangeably. Many manufacturers and others in the home-heating industry disagree about their meaning. For example, some manufacturers use the term *fireplace stove* to describe what others would consider an insert. Let me begin by defining the terms — insert, fireplace stove and conventional stove — as I understand them.

Freestanding fireplace stoves. These stoves have either glass or metal doors that open to the front, enabling owners to view the fire. They may be vented into the fireplace flue with a stovepipe connection. And these stoves often have many of the features of efficient, conventional stoves, including airtight seals and interior baffles. Fireplace stoves provide radiant and convected heat.

Conventional stoves. This category includes any conventional wood, or coal stove. Most often, conventional stoves must be operated with the doors closed, thereby eliminating the fire from view. Connecting an airtight, conventional stove to a fireplace flue can be an efficient home-heating installation. These stoves also provide radiant and convected heat.

Figure 5-1. Three basic, home-heating appliances suitable for fireplaces: the insert (top), free-standing fireplace stove (lower left) and conventional stove (lower right).

When connected by a length of stovepipe to the chimney flue, these stoves provide one of the best, most efficient energy sources available. That's especially true if they are airtight, have a baffle system, secondary combustion and a fan that helps circulate their heat.

Inserts. Typically, the bulk of an insert slides back into a fireplace cavity, and a relatively small part of the unit projects forward into the living area. Most good inserts have air inlets for primary and secondary combustion and blowers to enhance the movement of heat. Most are of double wall construction, which creates a "stove within a stove." Many inserts have firebrick liners covering their bottoms. Unlike conventional stoves, inserts are built specifically for fireplaces.

MAKING A CHOICE

When selecting from the many stoves, inserts and fireplace stoves, consider these factors:

- Appearance
- Efficiency
- Size
- Rated heat output
- Dimensions
- Ease of installation
- Safety
- Materials and workmanship
- Special features
- Maintenance and service

Appearance

How a heating appliance will appear in your living room is an obvious concern. There is an extraordinary array of sizes, materials, special features and colors to choose from (see Catalog, pp. 99–147). Most fireplace appliances are black or have a dark-metal exterior; however, some imported stoves come in colors such as dark green and maroon.

Fireplace appliances are also available in many different designs and shapes. Most are box shaped, but others have more innovative designs. Garrison manufactures a fireplace stove that is octagonal. Some inserts fit flush with the fireplace face; more often, inserts, stoves and fireplace stoves protrude into the room.

The prospective buyer must also select an appropriate style. All fireplace appliances have distinctive styles, made apparent or highlighted by the basic design, the trim, accessories and options. Some fireplace appliances would complement a colonial living room nicely; others would not. Still others would fit in a modern ranch-style home, where a more ornate design might be out of place. Appliances are available with or without blowers, cooking surfaces, doors, brass, copper and steel trim and many other accessories.

Take your time making a decision. You can use a cardboard box to simulate the appearance of the unit in your fireplace. Place it in various positions likely to be occupied by the stove you intend to purchase.

Efficiency

In the solid fuel industry, "efficiency" has many meanings and not everyone agrees about the way the word is used. But, when applied to a home heating appliance, I intend efficiency to mean the total amount of useful heat (measured in Btus) that comes out into a room, divided by the energy (or Btu) content of the solid fuel placed in the appliance. Those who test appliances to determine efficiency ratings are trying to arrive at a figure determined by dividing Btu output (heat) by Btu input (fuel).

On stove labels, these ratings (and other test information) are expressed as percentages for three heating ranges — low, medium and high (see Figure 5-2). Debate arises, nevertheless, because not everyone agrees about the methods used to determine Btu input and output. About 20 agencies and companies perform the tests for various manufacturers. And some manufacturers disagree about the validity of various testing methods. However, the results of these tests are consistent enough to enable some generalizations about inserts, conventional stoves and fireplace stoves and their relative efficiencies.

Of the three appliances, the most efficient is a high-quality, airtight, conventional stove, connected to the chimney flue by stovepipe installed above the mantel. Under the best conditions, such an installation can achieve an efficiency of at least 60 percent.

Inserts and fireplace stoves increase the amount of heat you get from

MODEL				
	WOOD LBS/HR	BTU/HR OUTPUT	% EFFICIENCY RANGE	CFM ROOM AIR REQUIRED
1.				
2.				
3.				

TEST UNIT EQUIPPED WITH ACCESSORY _____

These data were obtained under test conditions in accordance with the Fireplace Institute Standard 1-79 for wood-fired, open combustion chamber heating appliances, and may not be reproducible in home operation.

FIREPLACE INSTITUTE

Figure 5-2. FI label gives this data (for three different firing rates): wood burned, heat output, efficiency range and room air required (cubic feet per minute). No single efficiency label has been designated for all heating appliances.

your fireplace, but more often than not the efficiency gains are less dramatic. Typically, an insert has an efficiency of 35 to 55 percent, while a fireplace stove might have an efficiency of 15 to 35 percent. Still, there's potential for significant fireplace performance improvement. Remember, most conventional masonry fireplaces have a maximum efficiency of only 10 percent.

I think the best advice for the heating-appliance buyer is to ask a dealer or manufacturer for efficiency test results on a particular model. These will show how the tests were conducted and the methods used to determine efficiency figures.

Size

When selecting a heating appliance, one of the important questions to ask is, "What purpose will the unit serve?" In other words, how will it be used, where will it be used and how much space will it heat? Often homeowners purchase heating appliances that are too large or too small for their present or future needs. Plan ahead. Think about your heating requirements, not just for this year, but for the next five years. It is better to select a unit that's too small than too large because a heating appliance that produces too much heat may have to be damped down excessively, and that means more creosote.

Rated heat output. Heat output is another area of confusion. Fireplace heating appliances are rated in one of three ways. Remember, though, that the way an appliance actually performs will be affected by such factors as the dryness or quality of the fuel, the amount of air infiltration into the room, the nature of the draft and the outside weather conditions.

1. Some ratings are based on area to be heated. Heat output will appear as, for example, "Insert X heats 2,000 square feet." To match your situation with the figures for a particular unit, make a sketch of the room(s) you want to heat. Jot down approximate room sizes, location of door openings, stairs and fireplace. Take this sketch to a dealer or manufacturer and ask to see models with an output that matches your requirements.

2. More often, heat output is expressed in *British thermal units* or Btus. A Btu is the quantity of heat required to raise the temperature of one pound of water one degree Fahrenheit at or near 39.2°F. (As an indicator of Btu requirements: the average home is 1,200 square feet and requires roughly 100,000 Btus per hour to maintain a temperature of 65°F. in the winter when the outside temperature is about 20°F.)

3. A third way appliance outputs are expressed is in *cubic feet* or *volume of heated area.* This is the floor area to be heated multiplied by 8 feet (the standard height of most rooms). "Both this value and area heated assume some level of insulation and tightness to the home," says John Bartok, a solid fuel authority. "If you have an older home with little or no insulation and you can feel the cold draft on your feet during the winter it would be best to use about two-thirds of the figure stated by the manufacturer. On the other hand, if yours is a modern, tight, well-insulated home, you can probably add a third to the value and still have the stove do a good job."*

Appliance dimensions. There are some other dimensions that are just as important as the area or volume of room(s) to be heated. There are, of course, the dimensions of the appliance. To fit a unit to your fireplace — whether it's an insert or fireplace stove — you must first know the dimensions of the fireplace (see Figure 5–3). And, you must know how far an appliance will project onto your hearth and into the living room. In some cases, protective mantel panels and spark mats may be necessary.

Ease of Installation

Also important is the ease of installation and the amount of adaptation or change necessary for safe installation. The insert usually requires few, if

---

*John Bartok, *Heating With Coal* (Charlotte, Vt.: Garden Way Publishing Co., 1980).

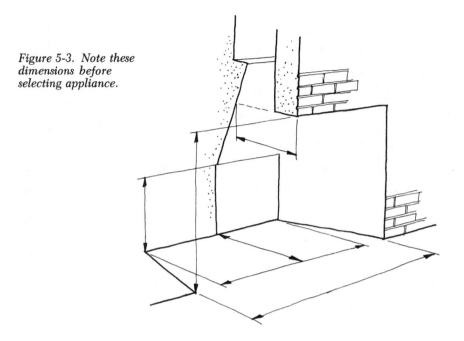

Figure 5-3. Note these dimensions before selecting appliance.

any, masonry changes and is easier to install than a stove. Most inserts have no legs; they slide into a fireplace box; and some connect directly to the flue. On the other hand, the conventional stove connected by stovepipe to the flue above the mantel requires a lot of masonry work and adaptation.

The weight of a unit is another important consideration that may affect the ease of installation.

Safety

To be safe, select a fireplace appliance that can be easily installed and easily removed for maintenance and cleaning. Periodic cleaning of the chimney flue is essential to avoid chimney fires from creosote. "Most fireplace chimneys are very oversized for most stoves," says Jay Shelton, director of Shelton Energy Research. "As a consequence there is often excessive cooling of the smoke due to the large surface area and low flue-gas velocity, and condensation, creosote buildup and low draft can result."[*]

Find out if there are any safety limitations on the unit or other factors

---

[*]Jay W. Shelton, *Wood Heat Safety* (Charlotte, Vt.: Garden Way Publishing Co., 1979).

that might represent safety hazards. For example, will the unit clear all combustibles by safe margins (see Chapters 6 and 7)? Are there any limits on the unit's warranty? Most inserts, fireplace stoves and conventional stoves may *not* be installed in prefabricated metal fireplaces. Others are not recommended for mobile homes. These are the kinds of limitations to watch out for.

Building codes. Check with your local building inspector and inquire about building and safety codes before installing a stove. After the installation is complete, it's standard practice to have the work checked by a building inspector. Also discuss a proposed heating appliance installation with your insurance agent to see if it will affect your homeowner's policy.

"Listed" stoves. Several states with state-wide building codes require that a stove or heating appliance be listed before it will be approved by a building inspector. Listing means the stove has passed strict safety testing procedures performed by an accepted testing laboratory such as Underwriters Laboratory. These tests differ from efficiency tests. Once a heating appliance has been listed, it is generally considered to be safe if installed properly.

Materials and Workmanship

The safety and performance of a home heating appliance — stove, insert or fireplace stove — also hinge on the quality of materials and workmanship. What is the unit made of and how well is it made are important questions to answer when trying to size up any fireplace appliance. The fireboxes of most stoves, inserts and fireplace stoves are made of steel or cast iron. Usually, cast iron is preferable because it does not warp as easily as steel, especially if the steel is thin. Cast iron also tends to be more resilient and able to withstand high temperatures. Nonetheless, some manufacturers prefer steel because it is less likely than cast iron to crack when sudden temperature changes occur.

Quality of workmanship is also important. In general, airtight appliances, well sealed to block unwanted air, offer the greatest combustion control and the greatest efficiency. Look for units with doors that fit well and close tightly; check for sealed joints that are welded or cemented together; doors with gaskets are usually more airtight than those without.

If a friend has a unit you're interested in, watch it in a darkened room when a fire is in progress. If the seals are tight, no light should shine through. Placing a lamp or flashlight in the unit is another way to make the same test.

Most good airtight stoves and fireplace heating appliances can retain a fire overnight (eight to ten hours) on a single load of firewood. In the morning a hot bed of coals remains, enough to restart a fire.

Special Features

Liners. Many fireplace appliances are available with firebox liners made of refractory firebrick, ceramic brick or fire clay. Liners add weight, and the heavier a unit is, the more durable it is. A heavy liner also protects the metal from burnout. Furthermore, the added mass of liner material retains more heat. By absorbing heat and moderating temperature extremes, a liner enhances the delivery of even heat to a room. Exterior fiberglass insulation, available on some inserts, is another feature that helps moderate temperatures while improving heat output.

Air controls. Air ducts, vents, and openings help to circulate and regulate air through a unit. These can be operated manually or in some cases may be thermostatically controlled. Often, a blower or two is part of the air control system. Blowers hasten the transfer of heat to your room.

Thermostat. A thermostat automatically adjusts the combustion rate in a fireplace appliance. This device may be available on conventional stoves as well as on some of the newer fireplace inserts. A thermostat senses the temperature of the air at the appliance and adjusts a damper to admit more or less air, thereby altering the combustion rate. An operator should be able to set a properly working thermostat once, then sit back and enjoy an optimum-temperature fire.

Interior baffles and chambers. The way air and gases move through a fireplace appliance can be adjusted by a thermostat, but movement and performance are also influenced by the arrangement of interior baffles and chambers that channel the heat throughout the unit. Combustion and heat-transfer characteristics of stoves, inserts and fireplace stoves will be discussed in more detail in Chapters 6 and 7.

Maintenance and Service

Ease of maintenance and reliability of service are two final important items. Not only must a unit be easy to install and remove for cleaning, it should also have durable parts that require little attention. For example, if you want steady convected heat, select a unit with a sturdy, variable-speed blower. You may want to ask the dealer to turn it on to see if it has an acceptable noise level.

Dependable service is a must. Purchase your fireplace appliance from a reliable dealer or manufacturer who has been in business long enough to make a reputation. It's prudent, not inconsiderate, to ask for the names of others in your area who own and operate the model stove, insert or fireplace stove you're interested in. Visit these people and ask them questions about their appliances.

For a complete checklist of items to consider before making your final choice, see the accompanying box.

A FIREPLACE APPLIANCE CHECKLIST

- ☐ Is the stove, insert or fireplace stove the proper size, with the appropriate heating capacity?

- ☐ Are the dimensions of the unit, especially the height, appropriate for your fireplace? Will it fit in the fireplace cavity?

- ☐ What is the quality of workmanship and materials? Is the appliance built of cast iron or heavy steel plate?

- ☐ Is the appliance airtight?

- ☐ Do the design and style complement the living space to be heated?

- ☐ Is the appliance warranted for at least one year?

- ☐ Can it be assembled, installed and moved easily for inspection and cleaning?

- ☐ Does it have a baffle system to improve heat transfer?

- ☐ Is there a blower with variable speeds and durable parts that can withstand high temperatures?

- ☐ Has the unit been tested for efficiency? For safety?

- ☐ Can the appliance be used with the type of chimney installed? Does appliance vent to the top or back?

- ☐ Can coal and other fuels be burned in the unit, as well as wood?

- ☐ Does the appliance have a large, accessible ash pan?

- ☐ Are parts and service readily available?

- ☐ Is a standard-sized panel included to help adapt unit to fireplace face? Are any other adapters required for installation?

CHAPTER 6

Fireplace Inserts:
Installing and Operating

Fireplace inserts are a popular alternative for those who want more heat from their fireplace. The concept of an appliance that fits in a fireplace and boosts heat output is not entirely new. Benjamin Franklin had the same objective in mind when he invented the Pennsylvanian Fireplace stove back in 1741.

Inserts were used through the end of the nineteenth century, but then dropped out of favor when coal supplies became abundant and central furnaces more popular. Not until the so-called "energy crisis" of the 1970s did inserts receive renewed attention. Homeowners rediscovered the insert as a way to boost their fireplace performance without significantly altering their living room. A good, airtight insert with a blower or fan can increase the heat output of an ordinary masonry fireplace up to five times.

Check the Chimney First

A careful chimney inspection prior to installing an insert (or any fireplace heating appliance) is essential. The chimney flue must be clean, well maintained and structurally sound. Typically, the installation of a new appliance means the flue will be used much more than ever before. When this happens, the likelihood of creosote formation increases, as does the stress on mortar and chimney liners. Excessive creosote might be the fuel for a chimney fire that could damage the flue and nearby framing. If you have any doubts about the condition of your chimney, ask a professional chimney sweep or fire department to make an inspection. (Fireplace maintenance is discussed in Chapter 9.)

When installing an insert like this one, it makes sense to pay close attention to the manufacturer's instructions. (Courtesy Phoenix Manufacturing.)

INSTALLATION

Installation of an insert can be simple, but a lot depends on the particular model and the exact method used to "connect" the insert to the fireplace flue. In most cases, installation involves little more than backing the insert into the fireplace cavity. Several manufacturers suggest making a direct connection between the insert's exhaust and the chimney flue. While the first method is easier, the second is generally safer. With a direct connection, there's little chance that smoke and gases will linger in the firebox, cool and then form creosote.

Remember, though, that the ways inserts perform — and the requirements for efficient, low-creosote burning — vary. So my advice is to consult with your dealer or manufacturer and follow his instructions closely. Also, make sure you are up to date on local, state or federal regulations that might bear upon your installation.* Contact your insurance agent as well to make sure your installation will not affect your homeowner's coverage adversely.

Follow These Steps

While manufacturers' instructions may vary, there are some generally-accepted steps you can follow when installing an insert with a direct connection to the chimney flue:

1. After inspecting your chimney flue and fireplace, unpack the insert, examine the unit carefully to make sure that all parts are included and in good condition.

2. Gather together tools and materials. These are helpful: a carpenter's level; screwdriver; pliers; masonry drill and bits; putty knife; adjustable wrench; and tape measure. Fiberglass insulation is often used to seal between the cover panel and the fireplace face; in some installations, these and other joints are sealed with furnace cement.

3. Cover the rug, floor and hearth with a protective cloth, blanket or canvas.

4. Remove all fireplace accessories and equipment such as screens and glass doors. *Remove the fireplace damper or secure it in an open position.* Also, if necessary, remove the damper handle. A hammer and masonry chisel may be needed to snap the bolts that hold the handle and damper.

5. To make a direct connection between the exhaust outlet of the insert and the chimney flue, you can purchase an appropriate-size adapter to run from the insert outlet to the damper. (In some cases, manufacturers provide these with their inserts.) Or you can make the connection, using techniques that are also suitable for stoves. For example, if the insert outlet is round, you can extend it with 24-gauge stovepipe then pass the pipe through a piece of 22-gauge sheet metal that fills the throat opening. When possible, extend the pipe at least 6 inches above the damper level, to help induce smooth, upward movement of smoke and flue gases. (For details of these connections, see pp. 74–77).

6. Check the insert to ensure that all parts operate properly. Test the

---

*Oregon requires direct connections between the heating appliance outlet and the flue.

electric blower or fan if included. After installing either a stovepipe or an adapter for the direct connection, slide the insert into the fireplace cavity so its outlet is beneath the pipe.

7. Level the insert. Many units have leveling screws located near their rear sides. Connect the stovepipe to the insert outlet or flue. Rotating the pipe back and forth may help when trying to slip it down over the outlet.

8. Most inserts have separate flanges or trim panels that fill the space around the firebox. Mount these according to the manufacturer's instructions. Openings or cavities between the fireplace face and the panels should be stuffed with fiberglass. To create a tight seal, glue strips of fiberglass to the back edges of the panels. (If you do not use a direct connection, it's easier to mount the panels before pushing the insert into the fireplace cavity.)

9. Check for sufficient clearances. The insert should be 36 inches from unprotected combustibles or should have clearances recommended by manufacturers. Often the mantel is a problem: You can protect it with a plate or shield, mounted 1 inch from combustibles, that reflects heat back into your room. Also protect the floor surface for 18 inches in front of the hearth, if it is combustible. Noncombustible millboard or mats made of metal or fire retardant vinyl can be used here.

OPERATING AN INSERT

Operating any fireplace appliance efficiently depends, in large measure, upon two important factors — the quality of the fuel and the ability of the operator. Remember to use dry, seasoned hardwood or another high-grade fuel intended for your unit (see Chapter 2). To operate an insert efficiently, it helps to have a basic understanding of how the unit works. Here, then, is a brief description of combustion in a typical fireplace insert (Figure 6–1):

1. Usually, the insert consists of a firebox enclosed in another box. Combustion air enters the *firebox* at the base of the unit (in downdraft systems it enters at the top). This is the air for primary combustion. Additional air may be introduced into the firebox where it is preheated for what is called *secondary combustion*.

2. Smoke and gases generated by the fire pass around a baffle system, if installed, before exiting. Baffles increase the length of the exhaust path; they also slow the flow of gases. This means more heat is cap-

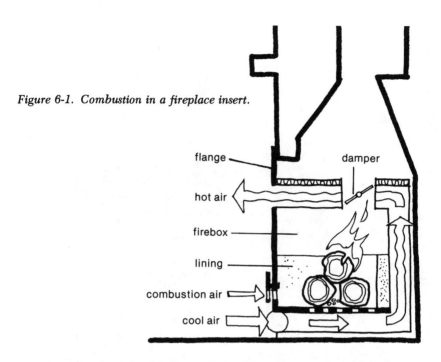

Figure 6-1. Combustion in a fireplace insert.

tured and retained in the unit (and in your room) and heat losses up the flue are reduced. Not all inserts have baffles, but those that do tend to be more efficient that those that don't.

3. Good units also have fans or blowers that hasten the air flow through the baffles and a double-wall chamber that surrounds the two side walls, the back, top and bottom of the insert. The blowers also increase the volume of heated air moving into your room. If the blowers are thermostatically controlled, the delivery of forced, warm air into the room is regulated automatically.

4. Combustion is also regulated by the vents or ducts and, of course, the insert damper. As you become proficient with your insert, you will learn the best positions for these controls, in order to achieve the best performance from your unit.

Getting More Heat
From Your Fireplace Insert

Each insert has its own peculiar or unique characteristics, so your manufacturer's guidebook or operator's manual is the best first source of information. In addition, here are a few general suggestions.

An attractive fireplace insert installed and operating in a colonial fireplace.
(Courtesy Garrison Stove Works, Inc.)

Before laying a fire, accomplish these steps:

- Plug the blower electrical cord into an outlet so that the cord will not be routed across the front of the unit or beneath the firebox doors (most units use 115 AC power).

- Open the air intakes and damper all the way.

- Place a wad of newspaper in the insert, light it and close the doors. When the unit and chimney are drawing well, the paper will burn quickly.

- Check for smoke leaks. If the draw is poor or if there are leaks, ask a professional to check your installation.

Once you've tested your unit in this preliminary fashion, it's safe to lay a fire in the unit. In most inserts, the fire should rest directly on the floor of the firebox, not on a grate or andirons. Wadded newspapers, kindling and one or two logs are sufficient for your first few fires.

It's a good idea to build small fires until the unit has "cured." Frequently, inserts and other fireplace appliances are coated with a paint that gives off a slight odor and smoke until after they have been heated a few times. Open a window slightly for ventilation until the curing is completed. Cast iron also needs to cure for at least eight hours (or as specified by the manufacturer) before it is subjected to extreme heat.

Once you're satisfied that your insert is ready for regular, sustained use, keep in mind these tips for safe and efficient operation:

- After making sure the insert damper and air intakes are open, light your fire and close the doors. Once the logs have started to burn, slowly adjust the damper and air intake knobs to obtain the desired burn rate and temperature.

- Add logs, one at a time, at approximately half-hour or one-hour intervals. This allows for a steady buildup of hot coals. Too many logs added at once will smother the fire or produce a smoldering fire. And this kind of burning is inefficient and unsafe — it results in creosote. Your aim should be a medium fire of even heat. Excessively hot fires that cause metal to glow are also unsafe and inefficient.

- With two or three logs well ignited, leave the draft controls wide open for about 15 minutes. This rapidly raises the temperature inside the firebox. As the temperature approaches 1,100°F., volatiles begin to burn off and the chance of dangerous creosote buildup declines. If possible, open the draft control knobs fully for 15 minutes each time a log is added to the fire.

- Once the fire has burned for awhile, regulate it with the damper and draft control knobs to achieve the kind of fire just described. The exact draft control setting for an extended or overnight burn is difficult to specify. You'll have to experiment to find the right setting. It will be affected by variables such as the draft in your chimney, the tightness of your house, the weather and the type of wood or fuel.

- Check the condition of your insert and flue periodically. When possible, remove the insert so you can examine your fireplace flue for creosote. Until you are familiar with the operation of your insert, the safest policy is to examine the flue weekly. Once you're sure creosote isn't accumulating rapidly, the frequency of these inspections can be reduced. Also check for rust spots, which should be removed with a steel brush.

- Dispose of ashes by placing them in a *metal* container well away from combustible materials. Do not place ashes in a cardboard box.

- If the unit has a blower, always shut it off before loading the stove, opening doors or emptying the ashes. If you spill ashes on the hearth, the blower might suck them up or blow them out into your living room. That's a real hazard—especially if the ashes contain "live" coals.

- Regularly check the condition of any moving parts, such as hinges, door latches, ash pan doors, glass gaskets, and blowers or fans. Leaking gaskets hinder combustion control, as do cracked glass doors. Most types of glass in inserts can withstand high temperatures, but their characteristics differ. Follow the manufacturer's instructions for cleaning and replacing.

CHAPTER 7

Freestanding Stoves and Fireplace Stoves

One of the best ways to get more heat from your fireplace installation is simply to block off the fireplace opening and connect a heating appliance to the chimney flue above the mantel. Conventional freestanding stoves and fireplace stoves can both be installed this way. A freestanding, airtight stove connected above the mantel can deliver up to six times more heat to your room than a masonry fireplace.

INSTALLATION

Connecting a stove to a chimney flue above the mantel is only one of the three ways to install these home-heating appliances (Figure 7–1). A second method is to make a direct connection between the stove outlet and the chimney flue at the damper level. A third method, which I neither recommend nor describe here, is to block off the fireplace face with a panel and then extend the appliance exhaust outlet through the panel and into the fireplace cavity. This last installation is not as safe as the others because it increases the chances of poor draft, low flue temperatures and creosote formation. While the above-the-mantel connection may be more difficult and requires the alteration of chimney facing, it is the safest, most efficient way to vent a stove into a flue.

Before you begin your installation, perform these important preliminary steps:

Check your chimney. Ensure that there are no obstructions or heavy creosote formations in your flue. Check the condition of the masonry.

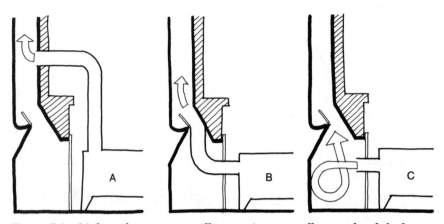

Figure 7-1. Of these three stove installations, A is generally considered the best, B is second best and C is least satisfactory.

Many pre-World War II chimneys were not lined. *Exhausting a wood-burning appliance into one of these can be dangerous.* If yours is unlined, or if you suspect it may be obstructed or damaged, ask a professional chimney sweep to inspect it before beginning an installation. (For more information on fireplace and chimney maintenance, see Chapter 9.) If your chimney serves as a furnace flue, I would not use it for a second home-heating appliance. In many places, local building codes will not allow it.

Check clearances. Make sure your stove or fireplace stove will be a safe distance from combustibles, such as walls, wood framing, mantels, plaster, curtains and furniture. There should be a minimum of 36 inches between any radiant heating appliance and unprotected combustibles (Figure 7–2). That distance may be reduced to 12 inches if the combustibles are protected. For example, you can protect adjacent walls closer than 36 inches with 24-gauge sheet metal, mounted on porcelain electric insulators so there's a 1-inch space behind the metal. Some authorities recommend a 2-inch space for even more safety.

If the floor is combustible, it also needs protection, and simple sheet metal is usually *not* adequate. Stoves with 6 to 18 inches of open air space between the bottom of the stove and a combustible floor require a good surface protector such as stoveboard (¼-inch asbestos millboard covered with 24-gauge or thicker sheet metal). The stoveboard should extend 18 inches on the ash-door side where hot coals could ignite the flooring and 12 inches on the other three sides. Brick, Z-brick, slate, stone, iron and cement board, installed alone, are not acceptable because they conduct heat to the combustibles below them.

Select the right stovepipe. Stovepipe should be 24-gauge, heavy-duty, black pipe designed for use inside the home. Most galvanized pipe is dangerously thin for wood-burning appliances. Six-inch-diameter pipe (a common size) requires 18 inches clearance, but this figure can be reduced by half if the combustibles are protected with a ventilated, sheet-metal wall protector. To go closer than 9 inches or through a wall, you must use stainless steel, factory-built, insulated pipe. The length of the stovepipe should be as short as possible. The National Fire Protection Association (NFPA) recommends the shortest, most direct connection between the stove and chimney. No more than two 90-degree elbows are considered advisable.

Collect necessary tools and materials. To connect a heating appliance to the flue above the mantel is going to require masonry work you may wish you hadn't started. If you lack experience, contact a professional and seek

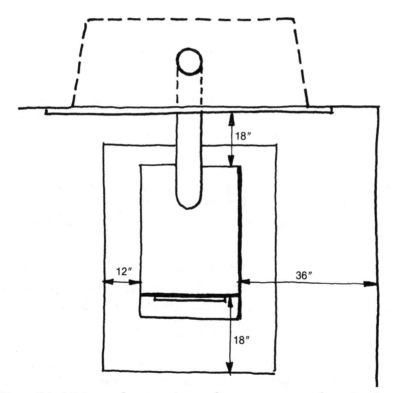

Figure 7-2. Minimum clearances for a radiant stove connected to a fireplace, and dimensions for protective floor covering.

help. However, if you want to do the work yourself, here is a list of tools and materials you will need.

Tools	Materials
electric drill with metal and masonry bits	stovepipe
	stoveboard
tin snips	damper
hammer	sheet metal screws (three #6 screws for each section of pipe)
masonry chisel	
circular saw or utility knife	furnace cement
screwdriver	fireclay thimble
pliers	

Connecting to the Flue Above the Mantel

This is a typical sequence of steps for connecting to the flue above the mantel:

1. Make a trial assembly of the stovepipe to determine necessary lengths. Determine stovepipe required for installation by measuring from the stove collar to the proposed hole above mantel. (Compensate for 90-degree turns.)

2. Cut a hole in the chimney masonry (and the wall, if there is one) above the mantel. If there is no mantel, cut the hole above the level of the chimney throat. Insert a fireclay thimble into the hole.

3. Close the damper or block off the fireplace throat below the hole at about the damper level.

4. Assemble and fasten the stovepipe permanently.

5. Connect the stovepipe to the heating appliance and place an airtight cover over the fireplace cavity. Recheck all safety clearances.

Here are the steps covered in more detail:

1. Make a trial stovepipe assembly. Position your stove in front of the fireplace. Then, beginning from the chimney, assemble stovepipe and elbows as necessary to reach your stove collar. To make correct connections, which will prevent creosote from leaking out, push the crimped end of one

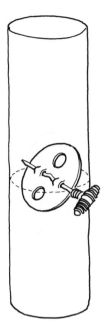

Figure 7-3. When installing a stovepipe damper, thread the steel pin through the stovepipe and the steel plate. Here, the damper is open; when closed or in a horizontal position, combustion slows and the duration of a fire increases.

stovepipe section down into the next. The crimped ends should always point down toward the appliance.

The appliance may require a stovepipe damper (many airtights do not), which is a plate with a steel pin and handle (Figure 7–3). To install a damper, first drill a hole for the pin in the appropriate pipe section. On most stoves, this is usually in the first section of pipe about 6 inches from the connection with the exhaust collar. Insert the pin and thread it through the plate. Press the handle so the point of the pin dents the opposite side of the pipe. This shows you where to drill the second hole. After drilling it, again thread the pin through the first hole, the plate, and then the second.

2. Cutting into walls and masonry. Unless you have an interior fireplace chimney, your first step will be to cut a hole through the house wall. Since most houses are of wood-frame construction, their walls are combustible. Consequently, the hole will have to be big enough so that your stovepipe is always a safe distance from the wall it passes through. Unsafe wall pass throughs are a common cause of home fires, according to the National Fire Protection Association.

If you should make a wall pass through, the NFPA suggests various safe ways to do it. Of these, the most feasible consists of single-wall, uninsulated stovepipe inserted in a fireclay thimble or steel sleeve, surrounded by not less than 8 inches of brick (Figure 7–4). The brick acts as an insulation, absorbing heat radiating from the pipe.

Without the brick, uninsulated pipe requires 18 inches clearance from

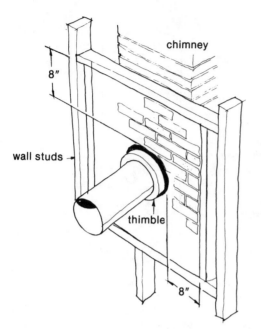

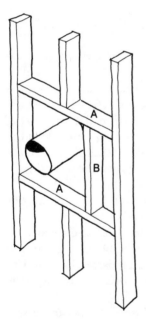

Figure 7-4. Uninsulated stovepipe, installed through a thimble and surrounded by a new, protective masonry facing.

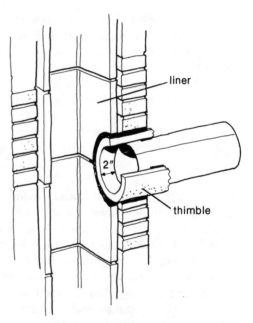

Figure 7-5. If reframing is necessary, you can use cross pieces (A) and a vertical member (B) to square off hole.

Figure 7-6. A cutaway view of flue, thimble and stovepipe. Thimble should be long enough to extend through new masonry facing as well.

combustibles on all sides. That's such a large hole (42 inches square) that the smaller pipe-brick installation is usually preferable. Even with brick, though, the hole for the stovepipe must be cut at a position that will keep the pipe at least 18 inches from *ceiling* combustibles.

I have not attempted a wall pass through (it's a task I leave to professionals), but author and builder Mary Twitchell* has, and here's the way she suggests going about it:

To begin, outline a square hole on the wall. For example, if you had a 6-inch diameter stovepipe, with 8 inches on all sides for the brick, you would need to outline a hole 22 inches square.

Paneling can be cut with a saber saw. Cut through sheet rock with a utility knife. Remove plaster with a masonry chisel and hammer, the lathe with a hammer and wood chisel. Also, you may need to cut out part of a stud with a saber saw.

Remove all materials until the masonry is exposed. Then mark a hole in the masonry that has the same diameter as the outside diameter of the thimble. The thimble allows you to remove the stovepipe for cleaning and inspection. (Check the inside diameter of the thimble to be sure it is large enough to accept the diameter of your stovepipe.)

With a masonry bit, drill holes at mortar joints between the bricks until one is loosened. Pull out the brick. Continue the process until all the center bricks are removed. Break the bricks around the outer perimeter with a cold chisel.

Between the bricks and flue liners there usually will be an air space which allows the tiles to expand. *Flue liners are fragile.* Avoid cracking them in the process of making your hole. You can use an electric drill with a masonry bit to make a line of holes sufficiently long to accept the blade of a sabre or reciprocating saw. With the saw, cut out the circle to the outer dimension of your thimble. Since fireclay will rapidly destroy both the bit and the blade, using a star chisel and hammer to work your way around is a better idea. They also are less likely to crack the liners.

Slip the fireclay thimble into the masonry hole to be sure it will fit. It should be flush with the inner face of the flue liner. If it extends into the flue, it will block the draft. Remove the thimble and set it aside momentarily.

If you cut through a wall stud when making your hole, some reframing may be necessary. Toenail crosspieces to the studs and end nail them into what remains of the stud you cut. Between the crosspieces, toenail an additional member to square off the opening at the proper distance (Figure 7–5).

Now, reposition the thimble and secure it (Figure 7–6). Cement the thimble using refractory mortar and spread to make a smooth joint. The special mortar is needed to withstand constant temperature changes. It can be made of one part Portland cement, one part hydrated lime and six parts of clean sand, measured by volume.

---

*Mary Twitchell is the author of *Wood Energy* (Charlotte, Vt.: Garden Way Publishing Co., 1978).

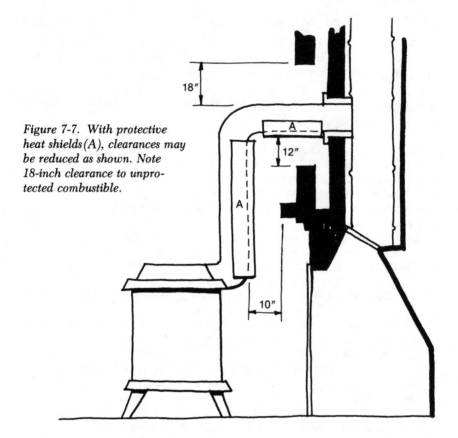

Figure 7-7. With protective heat shields(A), clearances may be reduced as shown. Note 18-inch clearance to unprotected combustible.

3. Block off damper. Close the damper or block off the fireplace throat below the hole you have made above the mantel. This will prevent room air from being sucked up the flue and interfering with the chimney draft. Be sure the closed damper or other blockage is sealed tight.

4. Assemble the stovepipe. Starting at the chimney, slide the stovepipe into the thimble. It should be easily removable for cleaning and repairs. Be sure the crimped end faces out. Then assemble the remainder of the pipe with crimped ends facing down toward the appliance so creosote will drip back into the stove. Sections of pipe should be secured together with three #6 self-tapping sheet metal screws for each connection. They may also be joined with heat-resistant sealant or furnace cement for further safety. If sections have to be reduced in length, they may be cut with metal-cutting shears.

Re-check that the stovepipe is secure inside the thimble. Squeeze asbestos rope or ceramic wool into gaps around the thimble to ensure a tight fit.

5. Connect the appliance. After the stovepipe is fastened, connect it to the stove exhaust outlet. Be sure that all joints are tight and that suitable floor protection extends to the NFPA-recommended distances under the appliance. Double-check all safety clearances.

Uninsulated stovepipe may be installed closer to combustibles than NFPA recommendations, if the combustibles are protected by heat shields. These can be mounted on the stovepipe itself with an air space between the pipe and the shield (Figure 7-7). Heat shields mounted on combustible surfaces also must have 1-inch noncombustible spacers to ensure the air flow behind the shield.

I'd recommend using stoveboard (¼-inch asbestos millboard covered with 24-gauge sheet metal, or some other suitable material) to close off the fireplace opening once the installation is complete (Figure 7-8). This board will help reflect heat back into your room; without it, some heat will linger in the fireplace cavity and be absorbed by the masonry.

Connecting the Flue Through the Damper

A second option, suitable for stoves with the right height to be vented through your fireplace, and easier than the through-the-masonry approach, is to connect the appliance outlet to the chimney flue through the damper opening. In this installation, the damper is removed or secured in an open position, and the stove exhaust is extended up the chimney to a point at least as high as the damper. The direct connection at the damper

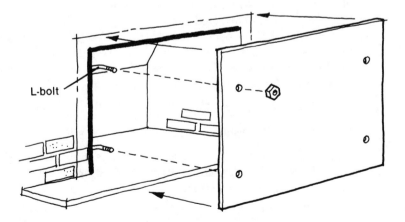

Figure 7-8. To secure stoveboard to facing, use four L-bolts.

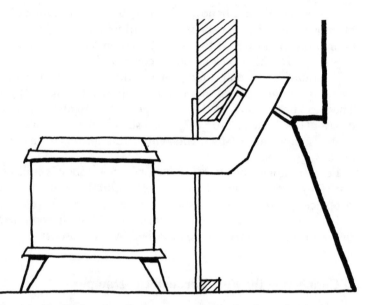

Figure 7-9. A stove installed with a direct connection to the flue. The damper has been removed and the stovepipe has been inserted through a piece of sheet metal. It may be necessary to squeeze the pipe to make it fit through the damper opening.

level is suitable for both stoves and inserts with round exhaust pipes or collars. Here are some ways to connect a stove directly to the flue:

1. Extend the flue collar with 22- or 24-gauge stovepipe, then pass the pipe through a home-fabricated piece of sheet metal that fills the opening left when the damper is removed (Figure 7–9). It may be necessary to squeeze the stovepipe into an oval shape before inserting it through the damper frame. If so, cut the sheet metal so the oval pipe will fit through it. If the damper opening (throat) is too small to accept the stovepipe, insert the pipe as far as possible into a piece of sheet metal mounted below the frame (Figure 7–10). Fasten stovepipe sections together with three sheet-metal screws at each joint.

2. Install an appropriate-size adapter, such as the one shown (Figure 7–11). This adapter was designed by Vermont Castings for its stoves with rear flue collars. Other adapters are available for top-surface collars. While some adapters are sold with stoves or other heating appliances, others are available as separate accessories. Obtain complete installation instructions from the manufacturers.

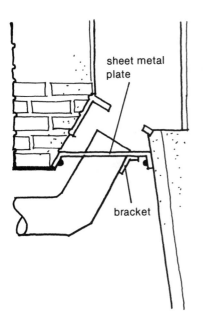

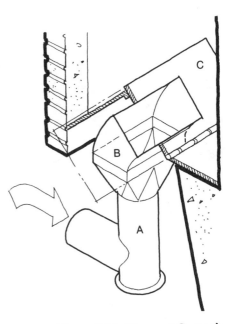

Figure 7-10. If the frame is too small, insert stovepipe into sheet metal mounted below.

Figure 7-11. Vermont Casting's stove adapter has a cleanout tee (A), duct (B), and plate (C).

3. Install a liner made of stainless steel stovepipe and connect the heating appliance to it. This is a relatively complex undertaking, but the end result is a continuous flue, a feature that should improve draft and reduce the chances of creosote formation. These liners are available from manufacturers, along with installation and maintenance instructions.

Here are steps for fabricating a sheet metal plate that can secure stovepipe at the damper level (Figure 7–12):

a. Measure the flue opening just below the damper. Add 6 inches to these dimensions, and replicate the enlarged flue opening on a piece of cardboard.

b. Cut out squares of 3 inches, from each of the four corners, so a 3-inch flange is possible on all sides. Bend the flanges slightly less than 90 degrees.

c. Place the cardboard into the flue to ensure that it fits tightly with the flanges facing down, toward the fireplace hearth.

d. Remove the cardboard and trace it onto a piece of sheet metal, 18 or 22 gauge, then cut out a permanent adapter plate.

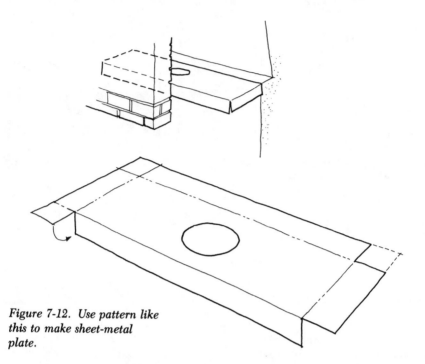

Figure 7-12. Use pattern like this to make sheet-metal plate.

e. Place the metal plate into the flue, to again ensure that it fits correctly. It should be snug enough to remain in place without attachments. If additional security is needed, use cement screws or anchor bolts. Caulk around the edges of the pipe and flanges with furnace cement to ensure an airtight seal.

f. If necessary, you can also use brackets to help secure the stovepipe to the plate.

You can install your stove so it rests either just inside or immediately in front of the fireplace cavity. In front is preferable because it allows for more heat transfer and convection. With this installation, it's best to block off the fireplace opening with a cover of ¼-inch millboard and/or sheet metal (Figure 7–8). Just millboard is sufficient, but the addition of the sheet metal will reflect heat back into the room as well as make the board stronger.

You'll have to cut a hole in the cover for the stovepipe. To make this cut, use a saber saw with a metal cutting blade. Secure the cover to the fireplace face with masonry anchors and bolts or L-bolts. Apply fiberglass insulation around the inside edge of the cover to ensure that it fits tightly against the fireplace face.

CHECKLIST FOR A SAFE INSTALLATION

☐ The stove or fireplace stove is listed or approved for use in your state.

☐ The stove does not have any broken parts or cracks.

☐ The stove is placed on a noncombustible floor or protective material.

☐ Radiant stoves are at least 36 inches from combustibles. If not, an approved clearance reduction material is used.

☐ Stovepipe of 22- or 24-gauge metal is used. Three sheet metal screws are used at each joint.

☐ The diameter of the stovepipe is not reduced between the stove and chimney flue.

☐ The run of stovepipe is as short as possible; no more than two elbows are used.

☐ For 6-inch pipe, there is at least 18 inches clearance between the *stovepipe* and combustible material. (NFPA guidelines call for a clearance distance equal to three times the stovepipe diameter.) If not, an approved shield or clearance reduction material is used.

☐ In above-the-mantel installations the stovepipe enters the thimble horizontally and does not extend into the flue. A tight joint exists between the stovepipe and thimble.

☐ A UL-approved, all-fuel, factory-built chimney or stainless liner is used when a masonry chimney is not suitable.

☐ The chimney and liner are in good repair.

☐ The chimney flue and stovepipe are clean.

☐ All seals at joints or plates are tight.

☐ A building inspector, fire marshal or insurance agent has reviewed the installation. Installation meets local codes. Smoke detectors and fire extinguishers are nearby.

HOW STOVES WORK

Conventional stoves and fireplace stoves are similar in several respects. Both can be installed using the same methods. Both are "freestanding," meaning they can operate apart from, but connected to, a masonry or prefabricated metal flue. And, both can be purchased with special energy-efficient features such as baffles, fans, thermostatic controls and airtight seals.

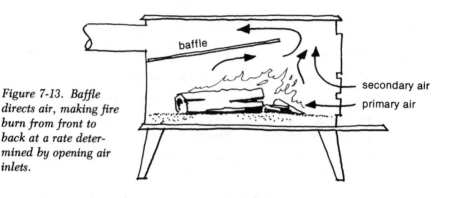

Figure 7-13. Baffle directs air, making fire burn from front to back at a rate determined by opening air inlets.

Conventional Stoves

Most conventional stoves sold today have airtight designs with adjustable air intake controls and baffling to enhance efficient combustion. A baffle plate divides the stove firebox into upper and lower sections and prevents heat from escaping quickly up into the flue. To understand how combustion occurs in a good, airtight stove, see Figure 7-13.

Air for primary combustion enters the stove through a lower air intake. As the wood burns from front to back, the smoke and unburned gases travel toward the back of the stove, then come forward along the bottom of the baffle. Secondary air enters at this point and mixes to cause secondary combustion of unburned gases. In efficient designs, with extensive baffling, a high percentage of the heat-producing gases is burned.

Fireplace Stoves

Fireplace stoves are distinguished by one prominent feature: they may be operated with their doors open, giving them the appearance of a "fireplace." One of the best-known fireplace stoves is the Franklin. Although it bears the name of the famous statesman and inventor, the modern Franklin bears little resemblance to Benjamin Franklin's famous Pennsylvanian Fireplace stove.

Combustion in a typical fireplace stove operated with the doors closed begins when air passes through the adjustable air intakes below the doors. It mixes with gases in the firebox chamber, and smoke travels over a slightly inclined baffle plate before exiting through a stovepipe. Fireplace stoves like the Franklin have dampers in the pipe, while many modern airtight stove designs do not require a damper.

Improving Stove Efficiency

Whether you own a conventional stove or a fireplace stove, there are some ways to achieve more efficient operation:

1. Add a fan. One of the best ways to get more heat from your unit is to add a fan; this will increase the volume of heated air moving forward into your room. (Fans that move 75 to 150 cubic feet of air per minute are adequate.) There are several good places to locate the fan (Figure 7–14). If you have an above-the-mantel installation, hang the fan beneath the mantel so it pushes warm stove air into the room. If the stovepipe connects with the flue at the damper, locate the fan just above the stove. Another possible position is at the base of the stove.

2. Seal joints and cracks. If you have a stove that's not airtight, or an airtight stove that leaks, seal all joints and cracks. Kits are available in hardware stores or stove stores that include gasketing and furnace cement for just this purpose. Although it's just about impossible to achieve perfect airtightness, the greater the air control, the easier it is to achieve efficient combustion. Furthermore, a tight stove won't be a sieve for warm room air when the unit is not in use.

When the fire is burning at night, turn off all room lights and look for spots where light shines through the stove. Mark these with chalk. After the

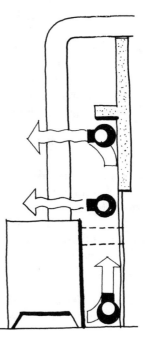

Figure 7-14. Here are three possible positions for a fan, installed to maximize the circulation of warm air from a stove into a room. The dotted line indicates the position of a stovepipe, connecting a rear-vented stove to the chimney flue at the damper level.

fire is out and the stove cools, spread high-temperature stove cement along the cracks and in the door seams. Press gasketing into the seams at the doors, then close them to compress the gasketing in place. Let dry for about 24 hours.

3. Build medium fires. The objective is to build a steady, even fire, with a 1- to 2-inch bed of hot coals. Every 30 to 60 minutes, add only one log. Don't smother the fire by adding too many logs quickly. A stove with a sur-face temperature of 400 to 600°F. probably has an inside temperature suit-able for efficient burning. That is a temperature near the 1,100°F. needed for secondary combustion.

4. Adjust the damper. To achieve the perfect medium fire, it's neces-sary to exercise good damper control. That means closing down the damper as much as possible without inducing a smoldering, puffing fire and with-out lowering the temperature so much that secondary combustion cannot occur. Many airtight stoves do not have dampers. Combustion control in airtights is achieved with the help of air intakes and vents.

If you have a stove with a thermostat, the damper is adjusted automati-cally for you. The thermostat senses the temperature of the air near the stove and adjusts the damper to allow more or less air into the stove. A ther-mostatically-controlled stove can maintain a constant heat output — or at least a reasonable range of heat output — automatically. It's a good instru-ment to have if you are unable to pay close attention to your heating ap-pliance.

Without a thermostat, it's seldom convenient to maintain a precise tem-perature or temperature range for extended periods. When constant tem-perature monitoring is not possible, try to achieve 1,100°F. for at least 15 minutes after adding a log to your appliance. That will be hot enough to burn off some of the dangerous, creosote-forming volatiles. Indications of good, efficient combustion include little or no visible smoke exiting from the flue and a fine ash left in the appliance.

5. Operate with the doors closed. Whenever possible, keep the doors shut. This recommendation differs from the one I made for conventional glass doors (Chapter 4). Most stoves are designed to operate most efficiently with the doors closed, so a tight firebox is created, damper control is en-hanced and excessive air and heat do not travel up the flue. In some cases, a unit is about twice as efficient with the doors closed as it is with them opened.

6. Add a heat extractor. This device attaches to the stovepipe and re-moves extra heat from the stove gases before they reach the chimney. In installations where a very short pipe is used or a hot fire is maintained, it pays to install one.

Extractors come in various forms. The simplest are sheet metal fins attached or wrapped around the pipe (Figure 7–15). Units are also available that replace a section of the pipe or fasten to the pipe in a vertical position. Heat extractors are *not* advisable for airtight stoves because the stack temperatures are cooler. A heat extractor would cause greater cooling and produce excessive creosote.

7. Keep the installation clean. Both the stove and chimney flue should be cleaned frequently and kept in good working condition (see Chapter 9 for more details). It is especially important to check airtight appliances or any appliances that have been operated with relatively small amounts of air. Under these conditions, creosote is a problem. Not only does creosote accumulate, it seeps into cracks and acts like a wick. If the creosote ignites, the fire might travel from these cracks into the house framing.

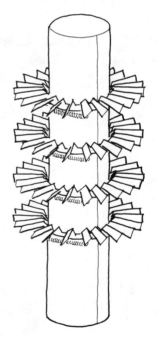

Figure 7-15. These radiating fins were designed by the Condar Company to extract and retain heat from stovepipe. Due to greater heat output, the company recommends that clearances to combustibles be increased to 24 inches, instead of the normal 18 inches for 6-inch diameter stovepipe.

Zero-clearance fireplaces may be surrounded by masonry or standard wood framing. (Courtesy Superior Fireplace Co.)

CHAPTER 8

Zero-Clearance and Masonry ("Russian") Fireplaces

The innovations and appliances discussed so far are suitable ways to get more heat from a conventional masonry fireplace. But also effective — and especially worth considering by those building a new home — are zero-clearance fireplaces, fireplace furnaces and massive masonry "Russian" fireplaces. If you're thinking of any of these choices, I'd recommend that you seek the assistance of a professional. My discussion here will be limited to an introduction of these alternatives and general guidelines.

ZERO-CLEARANCE FIREPLACE

A prefabricated fireplace that may be installed directly against a combustible wall is known as a zero-clearance fireplace (Figure 8–1). Its firebox is protected by an outer jacket or wall as well as an insulation layer at the back. Air circulates and warms in the space between the box and the outer jacket, and then moves out into a room, often with the help of a blower. And these features permit the zero-clearance installation.

Zero-clearance fireplaces are available in a variety of sizes and decors, with many features and options. Usually, they are constructed of heavy-gauge steel and they weigh about 300 to 500 pounds. The fireplaces are vented into stainless steel insulated chimneys or conventional masonry chimneys. Some zero-clearance fireplaces have ductwork that carries the heat into other rooms.

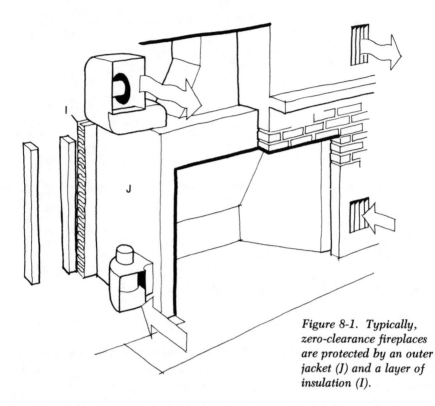

Figure 8-1. Typically, zero-clearance fireplaces are protected by an outer jacket (J) and a layer of insulation (I).

What to Consider

Here are some items to consider in deciding whether to install a zero-clearance fireplace: The manufacturer's warranty should be at least 5 years. Some units are designed to burn with the help of outside air. The ease of installation and suitability of ducting to bring this air into your home is another factor to consider.

The criteria for selecting heating appliances outlined in Chapter 5 may also be helpful to review before selecting a zero-clearance fireplace. The quality of construction, materials, style, options, accessories, ducting and appearance are among the items I'd consider. Most importantly — if the system involves ductwork, will it be compatible with the existing ductwork in your home?

Installing Zero-Clearance Fireplaces

Manufacturers of zero-clearance fireplaces provide specific instructions for installing their units. To achieve best results, follow these carefully, and, if necessary, seek assistance from a qualified heating contractor. Individual units differ enough so that it's impossible to present specific instructions here. But, these are some general guidelines:

1. Locate the fireplace against an interior wall to achieve maximum heating efficiency. Make sure the unit is listed by Underwriters Laboratory (UL) or by a recognized testing laboratory for installation with zero clearance against any wall or floor material. Some units are so listed; others may be installed with zero clearance from walls, but not floors. Some units must rest on non-combustible floor surfaces or materials such as masonry or sheet metal. Clearances are also required for the fireplace opening; it should be at least 36 inches from any unprotected nearby wall. So, be careful to determine exactly what the term "zero clearance" applies to before installing this heating appliance.

2. Prepare a noncombustible *hearth* of brick, stone or some other material, and extend it at least 18 inches to the front and 12 inches to the sides. This will protect flooring from coals and sparks.

3. Most units must be installed with the chimney specified by the manufacturer. Often these are UL-approved, double-walled insulated pipes installed vertically above the unit. Elbows or bends are not recommended because of their negative impact upon draft and combustion.

4. The insulated pipe should be installed with a firestop spacer to ensure a 2-inch clearance on all sides. The chimney should extend at least 3 feet above the highest point where it passes through the roof and be at least 2 feet higher than any other part of the building within 10 feet (Figure 8–2).

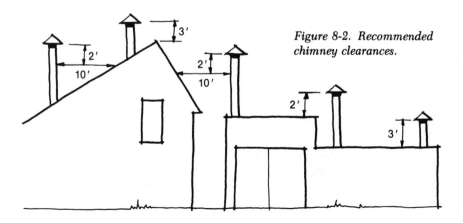

Figure 8-2. Recommended chimney clearances.

5. A chimney cap must be used to protect the flue from moisture which could corrode the steel chimney and fireplace. Before burning coal, check with the manufacturer to ensure that it is permitted. (Moisture mixed with the sulphur in coal produces sulphuric acids that are extremely corrosive.)

6. Be sure the system's fan is adequate to move the warm air out through the vents and/or ductwork and into the rooms you anticipate heating. To improve the flow of air, limit the number of right-angle turns in the ductwork to no more than three. Make sure all air inlets are free of obstructions.

7. Some manufacturers recommend that you securely tape fiberglass insulation around all ducts. If the ductwork passes through an unheated area, such as a basement, 2-inch-thick insulation is often recommended; 1½ to 2 inches is sufficient for interior ducting. Pack insulation only in places called for in the manufacturer's instructions.

8. Once the unit is in place, but not yet framed, light a small fire to test the fans. See if smoke draws properly. If there's any blow-back, check the air inlets for obstructions and check the chimney installation for clearance above the roof line.

9. Follow the manufacturer's recommendations on the choice of materials for framing the unit. Typically, zero-clearance fireplaces are framed with 2 × 4's, and the facing is either stone or brick. Obviously, the flooring and joists must be strong enough for this weight, and they may need reinforcement. Some units require a non-combustible "surround" (metal panel) that extends from either side and the top of the fireplace opening.

10. When installing the framing, leave access to the fan or any other accessories and their switches. If the fans are to be insulated, secure the insulation so it won't be sucked into the unit.

FIREPLACE FURNACES

A more sophisticated heating appliance is the fireplace furnace (Figure 8–3). In essence, this is a factory-built or zero-clearance fireplace that's been developed into a full system, designed to heat an entire home. The fireplace may be located in the home basement or ground floor. In a fireplace furnace, heat-circulating ductwork is an integral part of the system.

Fireplace furnace combustion is aided by outside air that passes into a

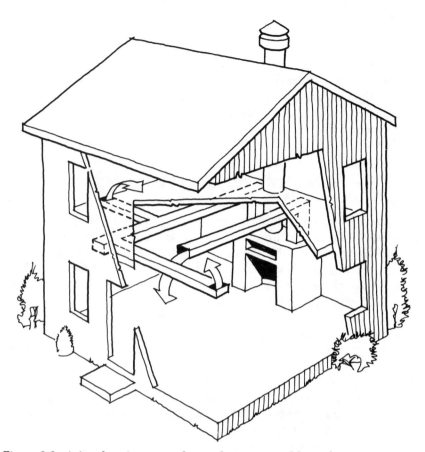

Figure 8-3. A fireplace furnace is designed to meet total home heat requirements.

plenum surrounding the firebox. Once the air is heated, it moves into the ductwork and out into the home with the help of thermostatically-controlled blowers.

Sometimes fireplace furnaces can be connected with existing ductwork. And there are also systems that tie in with hot water heating.

Fireplace furnaces have several advantages. Like a zero-clearance fireplace, the furnace enables you to view and enjoy the flames of a fire. Moreover, the fireplace furnace can provide even heat throughout the home. When used as a central heating system, a fireplace furnace may qualify for tax credits. For those contemplating a new home, the fireplace furnace could be a good alternative if abundant low-cost wood supplies are nearby. Many fireplace furnaces have twice or even three times the efficiency of an ordinary masonry fireplace.

On the other hand, there are disadvantages, too. Fireplace furnaces are relatively complex and expensive, sometimes costing as much as $3,000.

(I'd recommend getting bids on the installation cost.) Some banks do not consider a fireplace furnace an acceptable substitute for an oil, gas or electric system. They regard a conventional system as a requirement for home financing. Finally, most fireplace furnaces burn only wood, not coal or other processed fuels.

MASONRY ("RUSSIAN") FIREPLACES

Less than 150 years ago, large homes often had a central fireplace, two or three others on the ground floor and one in every upstairs bedroom. A kitchen fire was aflame 365 days a year. A huge amount of brick or stone was used to build these fireplaces and their chimneys. This massive heat reservoir was almost always located fully inside the home, not along an exterior wall where part of the heat might be lost.

Today, the concept of massive masonry fireplaces is regaining attention. Skilled masons in rural states, notably Maine, are building large, box-shaped fireplaces that retain heat long after the blaze has been left to wane. These systems, sometimes weighing several tons, are called masonry fireplaces, masonry stoves, "Russian" fireplaces, firestoves, brick stoves and probably several other names (Figure 8–4). Regardless of the name, the principle is the same: a hot, initial fire in the firebox burns off moisture and volatiles. This minimizes creosote formation. After about three or four hours, the fire burns down to a bed of red hot coals. The heat travels through an extensive series of baffles where it's absorbed by the masonry before escaping. In turn, the masonry gives off enough heat to warm a house for up to 12 hours.

Not only does the Russian fireplace give off steady, even heat, it requires little attention. Loading is necessary once every 12 hours. Like other heating appliances, the fireplace can be located in the basement for convenience and cleanliness. And a second fireplace, one of efficient Rumford design (Chapter 1), may be built into the masonry so there's a smaller source of heat for fall or spring days, when the full fireplace would be too warm.

There are some disadvantages to the Russian fireplace, however. After the fire coals are red hot, it usually takes from four to six hours to warm the massive masonry; conditions inside and outside the home influence the exact time required. To build one of these fireplaces, you must be prepared to hire a qualified mason and to pay a hefty price. Most systems also require a lot of space — such as 6 feet × 6 feet × 5 feet. Another drawback: even with a masonry fireplace in a home, another conventional heating source is usually required if you need to obtain a home mortgage.

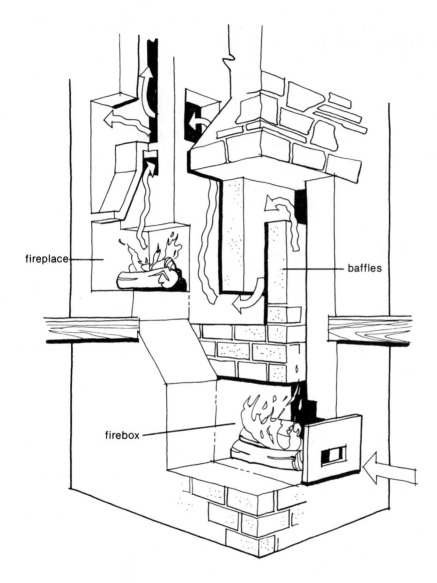

Figure 8-4. A relatively small fire at the lower level heats the Russian fireplace. As flue gases escape, they give off heat that is retained for hours in the massive masonry. A smaller fireplace built into the upper level may be used during mild weather.

Despite these drawbacks, a person building a new home might do well to consider a Russian fireplace. Several masons and owners of these fireplaces have reported good results — efficient burning with very little creosote. For more information and a set of plans, write to:

>Abbie Barden
>R.D. 1, Box 38
>Norridgewock, Maine 04957

Plans available. Barden also publishes the quarterly *Masonry Stove Guide Newsletter*.

>Basilio Lepuschenko
>Rt. 1, Alexander Road
>Richmond, Maine 04357

Plans and booklet available.

CHAPTER 9

Chimney and Fireplace Maintenance

Fireplace and chimney maintenance cannot be overemphasized. This is so regardless of the way the fireplace is used — as is, or with a new heating appliance added. With the new appliance and the additional burden it imposes on the fireplace and chimney, good maintenance becomes doubly important to assure safe operation.

One of the biggest dangers is creosote. When wood burns too slowly, it produces tar-like creosote that condenses in the chimney. If sufficient creosote forms, it can ignite into a hot chimney fire that can cause serious damage. To minimize this possibility, fireplaces, chimneys and heating appliances must be checked frequently for condition and cleanliness.

The frequency of these inspections and cleanings depends on many factors, including the way the installation is used and the quality of the wood or fuel. With wet, green wood, slow combustion, cold, oversized chimneys and light winds, creosote can form quickly.* Dangerous conditions can develop in a week. Under the opposite conditions, the likelihood of dangerous creosote buildup is considerably less. But no fireplace, chimney or appliance should ever be used for more than one season without a thorough cleaning and inspection. I'd recommend weekly checks if you are using your fireplace daily. The frequency of these checks may be reduced as you develop experience with your appliance.

---

*Studies at Auburn University in Alabama suggest that, under certain conditions, hardwood can produce more creosote than softwood. The studies also indicate that seasoned wood may produce more creosote than green or wet wood. These studies again underscore the need for frequent flue inspections, regardless of the wood used.

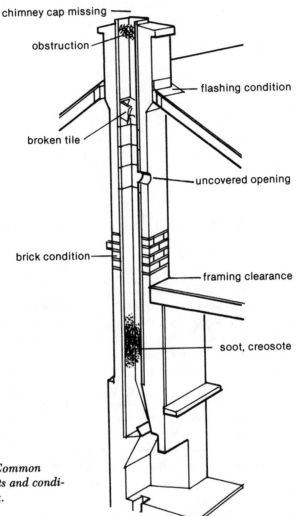

Figure 9-1. Common chimney faults and conditions to check.

CHIMNEY AND FIREPLACE INSPECTION

The need for inspection is especially great for chimneys and fireplaces that have been left unused for long periods, or that have been reactivated for a new heating appliance. Make sure both the chimney and fireplace can withstand wood heat. Some chimneys were built for stoves or appliances that burned some other, less intense fuel, such as gas-fired logs.

Once you've determined that the chimney can withstand wood heat, check it carefully (see Figure 9-1). If the bricks are crumbly, loose or missing, or there are cracks and fissures in the mortar, the entire chimney may need repair. Have it checked by a professional mason.

The best equipment for checking a chimney includes a hand mirror, a powerful flashlight and, for scaling the roof, a ladder and safety rope. It may be necessary to check the chimney both from below and from the rooftop.

In older homes, there are several conditions to watch out for. About one half the homes built before 1950 have no chimney liners. If you plan to use a fireplace frequently, it should have a liner in good condition. The joints should be sealed with heat-resistant cement or mortar. (If the liner is beyond repair or if installation of a fireclay liner would be difficult, installation of a new metal liner or insulated stainless steel pipe are other possible alternatives.) Make sure there are adequate clearances between the chimney and framing (2 inches is standard). Does the fireplace rest on floor joists rather than on a concrete foundation? That's another condition typical of older homes that should be avoided.

When you are on the roof, make sure there's a chimney cap in good condition, to keep out water that might mix with creosote and soot to form acids that would corrode the chimney. Water can penetrate, freeze and expand to deteriorate exterior mortar as well. Look for this when inspecting the chimney above the roof line. Look for any dark stains, signs that creosote may be seeping through cracks. Also make sure there are no obstructions such as tiles, protruding joists and birds' nests in the flue.

If there are small cracks in the chimney mortar, they can be repointed. Dig out the deteriorating mortar with a cold chisel and replace it with *mortar intended for chimneys*. Consult with a good stove store or building supplier for the best heat-resistant mortar to use.

Check also to be sure the chimney flashing is in good condition. Flashing is the metal stripping embedded in the masonry and extending beneath the shingles. Without it, water can seep into the house and cause damage.

Inspecting the Fireplace

Inspection of the fireplace is a continuation of the checks made on the chimney. A checklist recommended by Christopher Curtis and Donald Post, professional chimney sweeps from Stowe, Vermont, follows on page 94.

CHECKLIST FOR FIREPLACE SAFETY*

☐ There should be no cracks in any of the masonry, especially in the firebox.

☐ The hearth should be in good condition and should *not* rest on or be supported by wood or other combustibles. It should extend at least 12 inches on either side of the firebox and 18 inches in front of it.

☐ The ash cleanout door should fit tightly.

☐ Fireboxes should be firebrick lined.

☐ A mantel should be at least 6 inches from the fireplace opening. If it projects more than 1½ inches from the face of the fireplace, it should have at least a 12-inch clearance.

☐ Fireplace openings should have fire screens.

☐ Fireplace chimneys should have 2 inches of clearance on all sides. Fireplace backs should have a 4-inch space between the masonry and combustibles.

☐ Prefabricated fireplaces often depend on thin metal walls and air circulation to keep nearby combustibles safe. Corrosion is an indication of unsafe spots. Ash and creosote must not restrict free air flow around these appliances.

CLEANING CHIMNEYS AND STOVEPIPES

Cleaning a chimney is not an easy task, but it's an essential one. Whether you have a masonry chimney or stainless steel stovepipe; whether you use your chimney for an insert, fireplace stove or freestanding stove, cleanliness is in order.

Tools

To get started, gather together the necessary tools. You'll need a stiff, wire flue brush with a series of long, narrow extension handles. These remind me of the pieces of a fly fisherman's rod. The pieces are screwed together. The brush should have steel bristles that have a diameter as close to

---

*Christopher Curtis and Donald Post, *Be Your Own Chimney Sweep* (Charlotte, Vt.: Garden Way Publishing, Co., 1979).

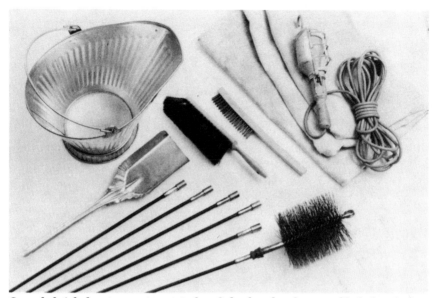

Some helpful cleaning equipment: shovel, bucket, brushes, trouble light, cloth, flue brush and extension handles.

that of the flue as possible. If there's a choice between a brush that's slightly larger than the flue or one that's smaller, pick the larger one.

Other helpful tools include a screwdriver to disassemble stovepipe, a large tarp or old sheet to cover the fireplace face while you're scrubbing the flue, a wire brush with a wooden handle to get into masonry corners, a shovel and bucket to remove debris and ash, a trouble light, a scraper and a pair of heavy-duty gloves. An industrial vacuum cleaner, which can be rented, is a most helpful, if not essential, piece of equipment for difficult chimney-cleaning jobs. When working on such jobs, wear goggles and a mouth protector.

Two Methods

A chimney or stovepipe may be cleaned from either the hearth or roof-top. There are advantages and disadvantages to both methods. Rooftop cleaning may seem a bit treacherous, but it's a good way to clean a flue. You can push the steel brush down from the top, then in many cases, clean the debris after it has fallen into the unit below.

If you select the safer method — pushing the brush upward while kneel-

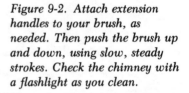

Figure 9-2. Attach extension handles to your brush, as needed. Then push the brush up and down, using slow, steady strokes. Check the chimney with a flashlight as you clean.

ing at the hearth — the appliance must be removed first. Both methods may be complicated by permanent chimney caps, dampers that have to be removed or bends in the chimney or stovepipe. You'll have to select the method that seems best suited for your installation.

Removing a stovepipe damper is usually not difficult. Typically, it's a matter of disconnecting the pipe at a nearby joint, reaching in and holding the damper plate, then twisting the handle free. Removal in a masonry chimney is more complicated and sometimes impossible! Usually, these dampers are attached to a support frame by cotter pins. Take these out if possible, or rotate them to free the damper. If you can't remove the damper, you'll have to work around it. (Before removing the damper, shovel your fireplace ash bed into a bucket. Return the ashes after your cleaning is completed.)

Cleaning From the Rooftop

Let's assume you've decided to clean the chimney from the top down. After removing the damper, or at least leaving it open, tape a tarp or sheet to the fireplace face, to minimize the chance of dust entering the room. If an appliance is installed, close all vents, doors and any other openings.

When ascending the roof, use a ladder, placed so it rests against the side of the house with a 4:1 angle. That means that for every four units of vertical measurement, the base of the ladder should be placed one unit out from the wall. If possible, have someone steady the ladder for you. You may need a second ladder to reach the peak of the roof.

If your chimney has a removable cap, remove it and place it aside. Next, attach the first extension handle to your brush and push the brush down into the flue as far as you can, using slow, steady strokes, going up and down four or five times. As you complete a section of the flue, add another extension handle (Figure 9–2). Continue to increase the length of the handle until the full length of the flue has been cleaned. Try to avoid damage to mortar as you stroke up and down. Use your flashlight to check the progress of your work.

After completing the brushing, find something to do for an hour or so while permitting the dust to settle. Then go back to your fireplace face, remove the tarp and shovel the soot, creosote and debris into a bucket. If you have an appliance connected to your chimney, this material should have collected inside. It may be necessary to disconnect the appliance to clean the lower chimney thoroughly.

CLEANING FIREPLACES

After you have cleaned your chimney, the chances are that creosote, soot or debris has fallen on the fireplace and the fireplace smoke shelf. If an appliance is installed, pipe sections connecting the appliance to the flue may be clogged. To clean this debris, you must remove the appliance. Before doing this, be sure to cover the hearth, nearby flooring and surrounding furniture with protective covering. Soot and dust are difficult to remove from furniture.

Most professional chimney sweeps use a heavy-duty, industrial vacuum to clean the lower chimney and fireplace. They turn it on and place the air intake so it can suck up loose soot while they're working. *Most home vacuum cleaners are not built for this use*. I'd recommend renting an industrial vacuum for heavy-duty, fireplace cleaning jobs.

Follow the manufacturer's instructions for removing your appliance from the fireplace. Once it is detached, rotate it to one side, so it's out of the way while you clean the firebox, damper and damper mechanism (if still installed), smoke chamber and smoke shelf. If you have a prefabricated metal, rather than a masonry chimney, you can clean it from the hearth, using your steel brush with the extension rods.

There are two ways to keep soot from falling on you: place your brush into the flue, leaving the handle so it extends out the bottom; then stuff a rag into the base of the flue. Another alternative is to tape a garbage bag around the base of the flue. Leave enough room at the top, or cut a hole at the top, so you can still push the cleaning rod up and down.

Once your fireplace is vacant, you can prepare to clean it. Presumably, ashes were removed earlier. Close all windows and doors to eliminate drafts. An updraft in the flue is preferred, so soot will travel upward and outward, not back down into your living room. You can determine draft conditions by simply lighting a match near the flue entrance and observing the smoke direction. If a downdraft persists, sometimes opening a window will reverse its direction. Another alternative is to wait until a cool day, then close all windows and doors. Under these conditions, the warm room air will probably seek the path of least resistance and escape upward, out the flue.

Use your hand wire brush to clean the firebox. Scrub away, especially in the corners, so no discernable thickness of soot and creosote remains. After completing this job, scrub the damper and damper parts clean. Do this step whether the damper is in place or temporarily removed. If you haven't already cleaned the chimney flue, this would be the next logical step. But, assuming that you have, proceed to the smoke chamber and smoke shelf.

If possible, the smoke chamber — the area immediately above the smoke shelf — should be scrubbed with your hand wire brush. Creosote and soot are likely to fall onto the shelf. Reaching the shelf with a shovel may be an awkward task (Figure 9–3) and it's another area that's best cleaned with a vacuum. Once the shelf and chamber are both clean, the task is complete. Replace the damper and ashes, and your fireplace is ready for its next fire. If necessary, reconnect your heating appliance.

Figure 9-3. Cleaning the smoke shelf is an awkward, but important task. Creosote deposits often accumulate at this point; unless they are removed, a dangerous chimney fire could result.

Catalog of Manufacturers

The following pages provide descriptions and photos of home-heating appliances designed for — or adaptable to — fireplaces. These descriptions have been adapted from manufacturers' product literature. For further information, write to the manufacturer or consult a home-heating appliance dealer. By no means is this a complete listing. Rather, it is intended to suggest the range of products available. Nearly all of the heating appliances have been tested by independent laboratories. In some cases, you can obtain test results by writing to a manufacturer. Results for specific products are seldom released to the public by a laboratory. Some of the better-known laboratories and related organizations are identified by these letters:

AGTL	**Arnold Greene Testing Laboratories**
BOCA	**Building Officials and Code Administrators International**
CABO	**Conference of American Building Officials**
CSA	**Canadian Standards Association**
ESI	Energy Systems, Inc.
ETL	**Energy Testing Laboratory of Maine**
ETL	**Electrical Test Laboratories of New York**
GA	**R.F. Geisser & Associates, Inc.**
GAL	**Gas Appliance Laboratory**
ICBO	**International Conference of Building Code Officials**
NTL	**Northwest Testing Laboratory**
PFSL	**Product Fabricating Services Laboratory**
SBCCI	**Southern Building Code Congress International**
UL	**Underwriter's Laboratory**
ULC	**Underwriter's Laboratory-Canada**
WHI	**Warnock Hersey International**

Allegheny Model A (Woodburner)

Allegheny offers wood and coal heating systems that can be used as radiant heaters, forced hot air circulators and remote add-ons.

The Allegheny stoves are radiant heaters with ¼- and ³/₁₆-inch heavy plate steel and cast-iron construction. They also function as forced hot air circulators with large blower systems. This high-velocity blower is mounted at the back of the stove and when operating is clean and quiet. The rheostat controls the variable-speed fan, which moves up to 540 cfm of air. The fan has an automatic off/on thermostat, and 8 feet of heavy outlet cord allow the fan to be plugged into any nearby receptacle.

The stove is of double-wall construction. Heat is blown out the chrome hot air diffuser located on the top of the stove. When the Allegheny is used as a furnace add-on, an optional plenum attaches over the hot air diffuser and ducts into your pres-ent furnace plenum for supplemental whole-house heating.

The double-wall construction of the stove maintains a cool outer wall for safety around children. There is also an inner safety heat shield.

The Allegheny wood stove is well adapted for use as a fireplace insert. The height to the top of the flue is 27 inches — low enough to be an "outsert" for a fireplace installation.

In the bottom of the door are the combustion air inlets which are adjusted by a convenient air-vent slide. The loading door is cast iron — airtight and removable. The viewing port is of high-temperature glass with a safety screen for added glass protection. For further safety the large 15-by-26-inch firebox is firebrick lined. A wide baffle plate, which slows the passage of the escaping gases, increases the amount of heat retained by the firebrick.

The four leveling legs are adjustable, and the wide ash apron makes for cleaner ash removal.

Company: Allegheny Stove Works
239 8th Street
Pittsburgh, PA 15238

Specifications:

Height: 29 in.
        27 in. to top of flue
Width: 30 in. at bottom
Depth: 21 in.
Flue: 7 in.
Fuel: Wood
Length of burn: 8–12 hrs.
Weight: 390 lbs.
Color: Dark brown and flat black
Safety testing: PFS

Apache Fireplace Insert

The Apache Inserts are available in 30- or 36-inch widths; the 30-inch insert fits a fireplace opening 32 inches wide by 24½ inches high. Both inserts are of airtight, double-wall construction for added safety and more efficient heat retention.

The quiet 265-cfm variable-speed blower is thermostatically controlled. It is designed to withstand 721°F. on the fan housing. When the housing reaches this temperature the blower remains at a cool 124°F., reducing the risk of blower burnout. The blower is conveniently concealed from view. It is mounted on the side of the unit for extra motor protection and easier servicing.

The front panels are made of cast iron to prevent the intense heat from warping the doors. Glass doors are also available.

The coil-type door handles remain cool to the touch because they are mounted on the draft control where it is cool, instead of on the door where it is not.

The Apache Insert has an ash drawer in the front for catching wood or coal ashes and for making ash removal easier.

Besides a 36-inch-wide fireplace insert, Apache manufactures freestanding stoves and hearth stoves, all of which carry a 7-year limited warranty.

Company: Apache Stoves
Route 4, Box 253
China Grove, NC 28023

Specifications:

Heating capacity: 2,400 sq. ft.
Height: 24 in.
Width: 30 in.
Depth: 19½ in.
Fuel: Wood and coal
Log length: 24 in.
Length of burn: 8–14 hrs.
Weight: 380 lbs.
Color: Black
Safety testing: Arnold Greene
Testing Labs to
UL 1482 standards

Aspen

The Aspen from Sweet Home Stove Works can safely and attractively convert almost any existing fireplace into an efficient heating unit. The stove stands only 23½ inches high (a smaller model measures 21½ inches high) and is 24½ inches wide.

The stove is made of ¼-inch plate steel with ⅜-inch reinforced doors. The bottom and walls of the Aspen are firebrick lined for heat retention, more even radiation and longer stove life. The internal baffling system reduces temperatures along the back of the stove while increasing heat output from the front and top. The baffle is easily removed for cleaning.

To vent the Aspen, the fireplace damper must be secured open or be removed; then seal the throat of the fireplace with a 20-gauge sheet metal blocking plate and gasket material at the lintel level. Through this the 8-inch (22-gauge) stovepipe passes from the stove to the masonry chimney. In order to ensure the proper draw, the chimney connection must be airtight.

To either side of the stove leave a 4-inch clearance space. This allows air to circulate around the firebox by natural convection without fans or blowers.

The Aspen burns both wood and coal and is loaded through the 11-by-17-inch door opening.

The stove comfortably heats 1,500 square feet and can hold a fire overnight. The 30-by-42-inch spark screen is standard and makes fire viewing possible; the stepped design of the stove provides a convenient cooking surface.

Sweet Home Stove Works offers an optional shield that is advisable if the stove will be within 3 feet of a combustible fireplace mantel.

Company: Sweet Home Stove Works, Inc.
1307 Clark Mill Road
Sweet Home, OR 97386

Specifications:

Heating capacity: 1,400–1,500 sq. ft.
Height: 23½ in.
Width: 24½ in.
Depth: 24½ in.
Flue: 8 in.
Fuel: Wood or coal
Log length: 20 in.
Length of burn: Varies
Weight: 335 lbs.
Color: Black
Safety testing: GAL and ICBO
listed

Atlanta Huntsman^R Fireplace Insert

In its 85 years of experience, Atlanta Stove Works has developed a full line of woodburning units, among them the Huntsman^R Fireplace Insert. The Huntsman is designed to convert a fireplace into an attractive, efficient heat source.

The unit will accommodate most fireplaces if the opening is less than 20 inches deep, 44 inches wide and 32 inches high.

At the base of the insert are twin blowers which move 200 cfm of air. Above the fans, the dual-slide, manually-operated inlets direct air into the combustion chamber which is made of ¼-inch hot-rolled, plate steel.

For the front of the insert, which is specially angled to reflect heat in a wide arc, decorative cast-iron doors are available.

Company: Atlanta Huntsman^R
Fireplace Insert
P.O. Box 5254
Atlanta, GA 30307

Specifications:

Height: 23¾ in.
Width: 25½ in.
Fuel: Wood
Length of burn: 8 hrs.
Weight: 375
Color: Black

Aunt Sarah AS 2

In designing stoves, Therm-Kon starts from a very simple premise: "You get as much heat from the fire as there is heated surface of your firebox and, of course, how much wood you load and how long it burns." Increasing the heated surface can be accomplished by enlarging the size of the stove or by incorporating heat exchangers in the design.

Since larger stoves take up valuable house space, Therm-Kon decided to design stoves and furnaces with heat exchangers made of heavy steel pipes welded into the firebox. The hollow, rectangular pipes increase the heated surface area without increasing the stove size.

The draft system draws cooler air in from the floor; as it passes through the two C-shaped pipes the air is heated. This heat, which would otherwise be lost up the chimney, reenters the room through the top vents in the stove.

With normal convection, Therm-Kon's Aunt Sarah AS 2 insert produces 45,000 Btu/hr.; with the optional blower, heat output can be increased to 63,000 Btu/hr.

The fireplace insert is simply designed. Two lintel draw-in irons hold the faceplate to the masonry. The irons catch behind the fireplace lintel, and as the bolts are tightened, the faceplate is secured against the fireplace. The leveling legs must be adjusted before a fire is laid. Then the fire is simply laid on top of the heat exchangers, which also serve as the fireplace grates.

Flue exhaust from most enclosed inserts cools substantially when it enters the fireplace flue. The Aunt Sarah open heat exchanger, however, burns more like a fireplace than a stove. Because the flue gases pass from the fire unrestricted, there is less, if any, creosote build-up in the chimney.

The unit is built of $3/16$-inch steel with replacable stainless steel burnout shields to protect the heat exchangers. The stove also has a manual draft control and tempered glass windows set in the cast-iron doors.

Accessories include glass cleaner, stove polish and a blower.

Company: Therm-Kon Products
207 E. Mill Road
Galesville, WI 54630

Specifications:

Heating capacity: 45,000 Btu/hr.
Height: 30½ in.
Width: 45 in. (front),
     23 in. (back)
Depth: 17 in.
Fuel: Wood
Weight: 220 lbs.
Color: Black
Safety testing: PFS

Better'n Ben's #801

The airtight Better'n Ben's combination wood/coal fireplace stove is made of ¼-inch boiler plate. It features ornate doors and a safety glass window for fire viewing.

The stove comes with a closure shield to block off the fireplace as well as a rear heat deflector to protect a nearby combustible mantel. The firebox is firebrick lined, with a cast-iron baffle and an ash pan.

There is an external shaker and shaker-rod fire-tender for use with coal. A 135-cfm blower is optional.

Custom-engineered accessories for the 801 include: baking oven, thermometer, coal hod and spark mat.

Company: Hayes Equipment Corp.
P.O. Box 526
Unionville, CT 06085

Specifications:

Heating capacity: 50,000 Btu/hr.
Height: 28 in.
Width: 21 in.
Depth: 15 in.
Flue: 6 in.
Fuel: Wood or coal
Log length: 16 in. (40 lbs. of coal)
Length of burn: Up to 24 hrs.
Weight: 310 lbs.
Color: Black
Safety testing: UL

The Cawley #800 multiple-use wood stove measures 26½ inches to the flue collar and is easily adaptable for a fireplace installation. The stove is of 5/16-inch cast iron, single-wall construction with a firebrick-lined base plate and an interior baffle. The single-wall construction allows for quick responsiveness. The firebrick base maintains higher firebox temperatures and cuts heat loss from the bottom of the stove. The top baffle protects the back of the stove by directing the fire towards the front and top of the stove.

The Cawley has draft controls on both sides of the firebox. The stove can be operated with both drafts wide open for the highest heat output, or the drafts can be opened alternately, causing the fire to burn from side to side.

The stove has a complicated draft pattern. Combustion air enters through an opening at the base and rear of the stove and rises through channels on either side of the flue. If open, the draft controls at the top of the channel allow the air to travel down, through a draft distribution plate that spreads air along the fire bed. This insures that combustion air is preheated, and the draft distribution plates insure that air reaches all parts of the combustion zone.

The Cawley #800 has a fire screen and large ash shelf to catch any errant sparks. The V-shaped firebox prevents logs or embers from falling out when the doors are opened.

The stove can be loaded through the large front door opening (19 inches by 10 inches) or through the 10-inch-by-10-inch side door opening.

There are two cooking lids that can be removed if you want to cook directly over an open fire. The cook rim around the edge decreases the chances that cookware will be inadvertently knocked off the stove.

Company: Cawley Stove Company
27 No. Washington Street
Boyerstown, PA 19512

Specifications:

Heating capacity: 55,000 Btu/hr.
Height: 26 in.
Width: 27 in.
Depth: 33 in.
Flue: 8 in.
Fuel: Wood
Log length: 24 in.
Length of burn: 8–10 hrs.
Weight: 480 lbs.
Color: Black
Safety testing: Arnold Greene
Testing Labs

Country Comfort™ CC700 Fireplace Insert

Country Comfort™ manufactures several freestanding fireplaces and fireplace inserts. All models are constructed from high-quality ¼-inch steel, welded construction, with no unsightly welds showing. All metal is chemically treated prior to painting to insure maximum paint adhesion.

Decorative cast iron doors fully gasketed for air tight fit, baffling and a firebox lined with firebrick are among the features of this insert. There is also a large removable ash drawer and a blower at either side of the firebox.

Country Comfort units carry a five-year warranty and have been tested to UL standards 1482 and 737.

Company: Country Comfort™
Orrville Products, Inc.
375 East Orr Street
Orrville, OH 44667

Specifications:

Heating capacity: 1200–1400 sq. ft.
Height: 24 in.
Width: 30¼ in.
Depth: 24 in.
Fuel: Wood or coal
Log length: 22 in.
Length of burn: 8–10 hrs.
Weight: 500 lbs.
Color: Black
Safety testing: UL

Craft Stove FP300

The Craft Stove is a forced-air heating system with a 265-cfm blower that pushes hot air out the four vents on the sides of the stove. The openings, two on each side, provide for more even heat distribution.

The blower has a three-speed rheostat. It forces the air through a specially designed baffle system over the heated area inside the stove, then back into the room. The blower is externally mounted on either side of the stove. Being in front rather than behind the stove, the blower is exposed to less excessive heat and is easily removed for storage or servicing.

The two door-mounted draft control caps spin so that you can finely gauge the amount of air for the most efficient combustion. The control caps are engineered to prevent sparks from escaping. Further protection is offered by the hearth extension, which lessens the possibility of damage from embers or flying sparks.

The double-wall construction of the Craft Stove creates a chamber through which the air is ducted. A baffle system in the chamber increases the air temperature before the air is forced out into the room.

When the fire is damped down, the wood burns more slowly and more heat is retained in the stove. The firebrick bottom retains heat and protects the bottom of the stove.

The ¾-inch-thick cast-iron doors will not warp, and the fiberglass rope around the edge makes the doors airtight for maximum efficiency.

Closure panels are available in any size and can be installed in less than one hour with just a wrench.

The Craft Stoves are individually built to assure quality of materials and workmanship.

Company: National Steelcrafters, Inc.
P.O. Box 56
Gastonia, NC 28052

Specifications:

Heating capacity: 2600 sq. ft.
Height: 24 in.
Width: 30 in.
Fuel: Wood
Log length: 20 in.
Length of burn: 8–18 hrs.
Safety testing: UL

Dare IV FP-24

Harrington Manufacturing Co. has test results for a four-bedroom, 3700-square-foot home that was heated for 12 hours by the Dare IV Fireplace Furnace on one load of wood.

The Dare IV fits fireplaces with a height of 25½ to 31½ inches and a width of 36 to 50 inches. The unit is made of ¼-inch steel plate with airtight cast-iron doors. Instead of the standard solid doors, there are optional Vycor glass door inserts 9 in. by 6½ in.

The two variable-speed blowers are front-mounted on either side of the firedoors; they pull 280 cfm of air into a mixing plenum before it enters the furnace.

Company: Harrington Manufacturing Co., Inc.
Box 269
Lewiston, NC 27849

Specifications:

Heating capacity: 80,000 Btu/hr.
Height: 37½ in.
Width: 52 in.
Depth: 15 in.
Fuel: Wood or coal
Log length: 24 in.
Length of burn: 8–10 hrs.
Weight: 546 lbs.
Color: Black with brass trim option
Safety testing: UL and Arnold Greene Testing Labs

The Elm

The Elm, designed and built in Vermont, is a unique blend of quality and practicality. The stove is available in three sizes to fit most heating needs.

It features a cylindrical firebox, ruggedly constructed from ¼-inch-thick cast iron. The firebox is held together with nickel-plated, cold-rolled steel rods which add an attractive touch. The firebox is firebrick lined to prevent burnout and increase heat retention. The interior baffle creates a long flame path which delivers more heat to the room.

The large loading door of 14½ inches in diameter easily accepts hard-to-split logs. The positive locking door latch and fiberglass gaskets seal the door tightly. On the fireviewing window is a cast-iron replica of an elm; the surrounding Pyroceram^R glass allows you to enjoy a view of the fire without sacrificing the efficiency of an airtight. The maple knobs on the door, unlike metal knobs, stay cool to the touch.

Below the window is the draft control which directs the air to the base of the fire for more complete combustion.

Also included as a standard item is a rotating cast-iron elbow which prevents burnout, a likely occurrence with sheet metal elbows.

The 45° rotating elbow can be positioned to vent the flue gases horizontally or vertically or to any angle in between. This means the Elm is easily adapted for fireplace installation. The fireplace damper should be locked open and the flue opening sealed off with a sheet metal throat plate into which an opening for the stovepipe has been cut. The stove can be positioned in or in front of the fireplace and is easily removed for chimney cleaning.

The Elm also has a decorative cast-iron cook top large enough for a teakettle or pot.

Company: Vermont Iron Stove
Works, Inc.
9108 Prince Street
Waterbury, VT 05676

Specifications:

Heating capacity: 40,000 Btu/hr.
Height: 25½ in.
Width: 23 in.
Depth: 38 in.
Flue: 6 in.
Fuel: Wood
Log length: 24 in.
Length of burn: 8–14 hrs.
Weight: 280 lbs.
Color: Black or blue
Safety testing: R.F. Geisser Inc.

Ember Hearth FP-50 Insert

The Ember Hearth Model FP-50 features double-wall construction with ¼-inch steel plate for the front, top and bottom; a ³/₁₆-inch inner wall; 1¼ inches of firebrick lining and a ¼-inch baffle plate.

The doors are solid cast iron with a fire screen for enjoying the warmth and beauty of an open fire.

On many stoves the air intake openings are *in* the firebox doors; on the Ember Hearth the primary air intake knobs are to the sides of the firedoors. This location prevents sparks from escaping through the draft openings. The primary intakes also preheat the air before it reaches the 17-by-24-inch firebox.

A central knob at the top of the unit lets in secondary air, which is preheated to 600°F. before it aids in igniting the volatile gases. The secondary air is evenly distributed through 32 outlets above the fire to insure combustion of the escaping gases.

The 465-cfm blower can be front or rear mounted. It draws in cool air that it directs up and over the firebox. The heated air is exhausted through 24 square inches of grillwork at the top of the stove. The stove also has 1850 square inches of unseen interior metal for larger surface area and therefore greater heat absorption and transfer efficiency.

The damper controls combustion by holding the volatile gases in until the heat has been extracted from them. As a result the Ember Hearth burns the fuel more completely and efficiently than some of the other inserts.

The unit is easy to install and needs a fireplace opening at least 25½ inches high, 32 inches wide and 20 inches deep.

The Ember Hearth has a number of safety devices such as the tight-locking firedoors with removable handles for increased child safety.

The stove comes with a 5-year limited guarantee.

Company: Southern Industrial Sales Co., Inc.
P.O. Box 8279
Chattanooga, TN 37411

Specifications:

Heating capacity: 2,600–2,800 sq. ft.
Height: 24 in.
Width: 30½ in.
Depth: 24 in. (with front blower)
    33 in. (with rear blower)
Flue: 4 × 12 in.
Fuel: Coal or wood
Log length: 20–22 in.
Weight: 420 lbs.
Color: Black
Safety testing: Energy Systems Inc.
    Results submitted to
    ICBO.

E-Z Fireplace Insert 36 CT

The E-Z Fireplace Insert comes in two sizes for easy installation into an existing fireplace. The EZ 36 CT fits fireplaces 24 to 36 inches high, 35 to 46 inches wide and at least 15 inches deep. Both E-Z units are of double-walled steel construction; blowers and glass doors are included as standard items.

Air for combustion enters the fire through the inlet in the door, then travels under the andirons that keep the logs off the bottom of the insert. In the back of the firebox are flat bar strips. They hold the logs off the back wall and permit the flames to travel back, then across the top of the fire.

The front-mounted electric blowers are rheostat controlled. When the air reaches 200°F. the 400-cfm fans turn on. They are located at the bottom of the stove to draw in the coolest air in the room, which cools the fan motor and wiring.

The fans move the air under the andirons. It then travels behind the back wall of the firebox and the flat bar strips.

Company: A-B Fabricators, Inc.
P.O. Box 8867
Greensboro, NC 27410

Specifications:

Heating capacity: 40,000 Btu/hr.
Height: 27 in.
Width: 36 in.
Depth: 15 in.
Fuel: Wood or coal
Log length: 24 in.
Length of burn: 4–12 hrs.
Weight: 502 lbs.
Color: Black
Safety testing: UL

Findlay Insert

The Canadian Findlay Fireplace Insert converts an open fire into an efficient convection heat exchanger. The insert works by natural air flow patterns. Cool air is drawn through the louvers to both sides of the firebox. The air then passes through a heat chamber where a built-in baffle system directs it along the side of the stove. Once heated, it is returned to the room.

The unit is of airtight, all-steel construction to provide more heat from your fireplace. The open base lets you use the fireplace ash dump, while the glass doors preserve the cheeriness of an open fire.

Below the glass fire door is the manual draft to give you maximum control over the rate of combustion and heat output.

Installation of the insert is simple. There is no masonry work, and the Findlay fits most fireplaces. The fireplace should be cleaned and the damper removed before installing the insert. Then slide it into the opening and adjust the rear leveling bolts. To install the insulation, pull the insert out slightly. Fit the insulation into the front plate and slide the insert back into place.

The insulation provides a seal between the fireplace and the insert front plate. There are four models that fit most fireplaces.

The 9-inch top of the insert provides a convenient cooking surface.

Company: Findlay Comfort Systems
107 Manitou Drive
Kitchener, Ontario
Ontario, Canada N2C 1L4

Specifications:

Height: 24 in.
Width: 28–36 in.
Depth: 17 in. (bottom), 13 in. (top)
Fuel: Wood
Color: Black
Safety testing: ULC

The Free Heat Machine

Instead of a contained firebox, the Free Heat Machine has 12 heat exchange tubes that also serve as a fire grate. The C-shaped tubes are made of corrosion- and heat-resistant steel. They offer 24 square feet of heat transfer surface and remain relatively cool because heat is blown through them by the two variable-speed, thermostatically controlled blowers.

The blowers are built into either side of the console. They have air intake filters to remove dust and dirt from the air. The filtered air then travels under, behind and over the fire in the heat exchange tubes.

A speed control switch allows you to regulate the amount of warm air entering the room. Clean, filtered air goes into the room; smoke and gases go up the chimney.

The glass doors for fire-viewing are mounted in antique brass frames.

Company: Aquappliances, Inc.
135 Sunshine Lane
San Marcos, CA 92069

Specifications:

Heating capacity: 90,000 Btu/hr.
Height: 20½ in.
Width: 25 in. (front)
24½ in. (rear)
Depth: 17 in. (top)
19 in. (bottom)
Fuel: Any solid fuel
Log length: 30 in.
Length of burn: 4–6 hrs.
Weight: 150 lbs.
Color: Black with glass doors
trimmed in antique brass
finish
Safety testing: UL and CSA

114

The Frontier FI-24-8 Fireplace Insert

The Frontier Fireplace Insert is durable and attractive. It requires no structural adjustments for installation into an existing fireplace and as a heat source will make a traditional fireplace three to four times more efficient.

The Frontier is designed without a bottom to take advantage of existing firebrick, fireplace ash dump and gas jet log lighters, if you already have them.

Loading the insert with wood through the 19½-by-9¾-inch firebox opening is an easy task, and the 7-inch hearth extension makes cleaning ashes simple. The stove can be operated with the custom-fitted double doors open and the black safety screen set in place for fire viewing.

Company: Energy Resource
Distributing Inc.
P.O. Box 2646
630 Garfield
Eugene, OR 97402

Specifications:

Heating capacity: 1500 sq. ft.
Height: 30¼ in. (face),
     23¼ in. (box)
Width: 42¼ in. (face), 25 in. (box)
Depth: 20½ in. (bottom),
     15 in. (top)
Flue: 8 in.
Fuel: Wood
Weight: 360 lbs.
Color: Black

Fuego III^R Fireplace Insert/Model A

The Fuego Fireplace Insert operates on natural convection and burns two-thirds less wood than an ordinary fireplace. It uses neither fans nor blowers.

Once the fire is lit an air flow begins. Room air is drawn in beneath the unit and is heated as it circulates around the hot firebox. After it passes over the back of the unit, the hot air is vented back into the room.

An insulated sealing plate prevents heat loss up the chimney. Heat loss is further prevented by the damper, which should be 92 percent closed while the fire is burning. The fingertip control is located on the front of the unit.

Tempered-glass doors contain the sparks and smoke while letting you enjoy the beauty of the fire.

The Fuego has a decorative grille that is installed flush with the fireplace opening. There is no hearth, so nothing protrudes into your room to take up valuable space.

A specially designed grate is standard and tilts the logs towards the back of the unit to prevent their rolling out.

Company: El Fuego Corporation
30 Lafayette Square
Vernon, CT 06066

Specifications:

Heating capacity: 42,000 Btu/hr.
Height: 24 in.
Width: 37¾ in.
Fuel: Wood
Weight: 140 lbs.
Color: Black
Safety testing: UL, ICBO, BOCA
and SBCCI

The Greenbriar Fireplace/Wood Stove

The Greenbriar is a unique, architect-designed woodstove. Although it is a freestanding stove, it can be top or rear vented for installation in a fireplace. However, the masonry flue must be at least 8 inches square.

Standard items with the Greenbriar include 11- and 14-gauge steel construction, firebrick liners and a Pyrex glass door. The hemicycle of glass measures 23 inches by 10 inches; if you prefer, a solid steel door is available. The door is hinged along the bottom and is easily removable for open fireplace operation.

To hide the four legs which support the firebox, Greenbriar offers an optional skirt. The skirt creates a pedestal-type base to facilitate cleaning around the stove. For increased safety an optional clearance reduction shield can be installed on the back of the stove with 1-inch spacers. The shield permits clearance distances to be safely reduced from 36 inches to 18 inches.

A further option is the hydronic system. An exchanger is installed in the fire chamber just below the flue outlet. Water is pumped through piping into the exchanger where it gains up to 30,000 Btu/hr. The heated water can then be circulated through the radiators of an existing hydronic system. An aquastat controls the pump which, depending on the stove temperature, will circulate the water through the exchanger.

Greenbriar Products also offers the option of an outside air inlet to let the stove draw its combustion air from outside the house.

Company: Greenbriar Products Inc.
Spring Green, WI 53588

Specifications:

Heating capacity: 75,000 Btu/hr.
Height: 36 in.
Width: 38 in.
Depth: 20 in.
Flue: 8 in.
Fuel: Wood
Log length: 30 in.
Weight: 225 lbs.
Color: Black

Grizzly Fireplace Insert FPI-1

The Grizzly Fireplace Insert is available in three sizes to fit most fireplaces and can be installed in less than one hour. With the leg kits, the Grizzlies can also be used as freestanding stoves.

The inserts are only top vented. Before purchasing the unit, calculate carefully to be sure the insert model will fit in your fireplace opening. If you wish to have the insert in front of the fireplace, add the height of a stovepipe elbow to the height of the unit at the top of the collar. Remember also to add the thickness of the floor protection and allow ¼-inch rise for every running foot of pipe.

The insert is of double-wall construction with two fans that blow air up between the walls and out the two side, hot air outlets. The fans are thermostatically controlled to turn on at 130°F. and off at 110°F.

The loading doors are cast iron; on the medium and larger models, glass doors are available. Draft-control knobs are mounted in the doors.

The stove is fireclay lined for longer radiant heat output.

In addition to the optional leg kits, Derco also offers fire screens and silver paint, should you prefer painted doors.

Company: Derco, Inc.
P.O. Box 9
Blissfield, MI 49228

Specifications:

Heating capacity: 1500 sq. ft.
Height: 22 in.
Width: 28 in.
Depth: 23 in.
Fuel: Wood
Log length: 18 in.
Length of burn: 8–10 hrs.
Weight: 382 lbs.
Color: Black
Safety testing: Arnold Greene
Testing Labs

Hearthside

According to the manufacturers, installing the Carmor Hearthside is as simple as positioning "the steel panel across your present working fireplace and connecting your Carmor stove."

The stove comes with a fireplace shield through which the stove is vented with stovepipe that runs up to the damper opening. (The placement of the stove in the room can be adjusted by adding or subtracting stovepipe.) The converter panels come in two sizes: 38½ × 33¾ inches and 46½ × 33¾ inches.

The firebox of the Hearthside is firebrick lined, and unlike most stoves, which work on an up-draft principle, the Hearthside is a downdrafter. The draft is regulated by adjusting two discs on top of the stove. The incoming air forces the gases down through the coals. Consequently, laying a fire in a downdrafter is slightly different.

Larger logs should be placed in the stove first, then kindling and crumpled newspaper. Be sure most of the newspaper is located under the draft inlets.

Company: Carmor Mfg. Co. Ltd.
325 Hale Street
London, Ontario
N5W 1G3 Canada

Specifications:

Heating capacity: 40,000 Btu/hr.
Height: 24⅝ in.
Width: 17⅝ in.
Flue: 6 in.
Fuel: Wood
Log length: 16 in.
Length of burn: 8–10 hrs.
Weight: 205 lbs.
Color: Black
Safety testing: Warnock-Hersey to
ULC #1482

The Hearthstone II

The Hearthstone II is an elegant freestanding stove with an outer layer of soapstone on the top and sides designed to increase the stove's heat-retaining quality. The stove is specially designed with a low flue collar height and narrow profile for easy fireplace adaptation.

Soapstone absorbs, holds and radiates heat more effectively than any other material—natural or man-made, the Hearthstone Corporation says. The stove is available in an attractive natural grey or glazed black.

The stove was designed to burn either coal or wood effectively. The Hearthstone II can be converted easily from wood to coal, or vice versa—right in your home.

Air enters through a thermostatically-controlled inlet at the back of the stove. To preheat the air, it is forced down the back of the stove and along both sides of the firebox where it enters the combustion zone. Or the air may travel along the back of the stove until it exits through a series of secondary air inlets. This secondary air is preheated to aid in burning the volatile gases that would otherwise leave the stove as waste heat.

Smoke and whatever unburned gases leave the combustion zone travel along the smoke baffle which runs the length of the firebox. An adjustable damper then directs the exhaust through a series of heat transfer fins. Here further waste heat is picked up before the unburned gases and smoke exit through the exhaust flue.

Hearthstone offers buyers a five-year warranty and this guarantee: if, within a 30-day trial period, they are not satisfied with the stove for any reason they may return it for a full refund.

Company: Hearthstone Corporation
Northgate Plaza
Morrisville, VT 05661

Specifications:

Height: 26"
Width: 27"
Depth: 21"
Flue: 6"
Fuel: Wood or coal
Log length: 21"
Length of burn: 12 hrs. (wood);
18 hrs. (coal)
Weight: 475 lbs.
Color: Black, grey
Safety Testing: UL

Hearthstove™ by Sierra^R 1200 Contemporary

The Hearthstove™ can be an efficient and attractive fireplace insert or a freestanding stove because top and rear venting positions are possible. When rear vented, the stove is 24 inches to the top of the flue collar. As a fireplace insert, the stove is designed to set on a 16-inch fireplace hearth.

The Hearthstove™ is made of heavy, ¼-inch plate steel with a sloping front design which throws more heat into the room. The stove is also raised on a pedestal for further stability.

The rib-reinforced, cast-iron firedoors are fitted with fiberglass instead of asbestos to insure a safe, tight seal. The stove also has glass windows. The glass can withstand impact and thermal shock, which is important should you hit the glass with a snowy log.

The firedoors provide an 18½-by-

10-inch opening. Each door features spin-knob draft regulators.

Company: Sierra
P.O. Box 1089
Harrisonburg, VA 22801

Specifications:

Heating capacity: 1,500 sq. ft.
Height: 25 in.
Width: 15¾ in.
Depth: 25 in.
Flue: 6 in.
Fuel: Wood
Log length: 20 in.
Length of burn: 6–10 hrs.
Weight: 330 lbs.
Color: Black, blue, green, brown
Safety testing: Arnold Greene
Testing Labs, UL

The Insider 30

The Insider slides into the fireplace without drilling or bolting it into place. The unit includes two side closure plates and a top closure plate to fit a masonry opening 25–30 inches high, 31–36 inches wide and 17 inches deep. The insert is of double-walled construction with airtight, gasketed glass doors that are tested to 1600°F.

There is a circulation blower system with two fans (200 cfm total) for optimal heat transfer.

The Insider's solid brass trim beautifully accentuates the lines of the stove, and the wooden knobbed firedoor handles are always cool to touch.

The Insider has a large firedoor opening (15⅜ inches high by 26⅝ inches wide) and a firebox capacity of 2.5 cubic feet.

Company: National Stove Works
Howe Caverns Road
Cobleskill, NY 12403

Specifications:

Heating capacity: 65,000 Btu/hr.
Height: 23 in.
Width: 31 in.
Depth: 27½ in.
Fuel: Wood
Log length: 16–24 in.
Weight: 330 lbs.
Color: Black with brass trim
Safety testing: UL

The Leyden Hearth

The Leyden Hearth is designed for those who want more efficiency from their fireplaces, while retaining a good view of the fire. The hearth has doors with large, high-temperature glass windows.

The unit operates on the principle of natural convection. It is not factory equipped with a fan, but a variable, transverse fan is available as an option. This quiet fan increases heat output by more than 20 percent.

The Leyden Energy Conservation Corporation warranties any metal portion of the hearth to be free of defects in materials and workmanship. Under Leyden's limited 20-year warranty, the corporation also agrees to repair or replace the product (at its own option), if operational failure occurs in normal use because of defects in materials and workmanship.

Leyden also markets an optional anthracite burning component for its hearth. This component fits into all Leyden Hearths, allowing owners to choose between coal or wood through-out the heating season. This feature enables owners to burn a full load of coal that will last through the night.

Company: Leyden Energy Conservation Co. Brattleboro Road Leyden, MA 01337

Specifications:

Heating capacity: 50,000 Btu/hr.
Height: 26 in.
Width: 26 in.
Depth: 17 in. (top); 20 in. (bottom)
Fuel: wood or coal (with optional component)
Log length: 24 in.
Length of burn: 6 hours (wood); overnight (coal)
Weight: 260 lbs.
Color: Black
Safety testing: Arnold Green Testing Labs to UL 1482 and 737 Standards

Liberty Bell Fireplace Insert Model 7901

Liberty Bell makes fireplace inserts and freestanding stoves that burn either coal or wood. The inserts are installed without any alteration to the masonry. No extra fittings or stovepipe are needed.

Liberty Bell's woodburning insert has a ¼-inch welded steel body with custom-fitted, cast-iron door and stove front. The door and frame form a tight seal to allow air to enter only through the controlled draft intake. A positive cam action latch and a full perimeter door seal help to reduce air leaks. The 12-by-15-inch door opening is convenient for loading large logs.

The damper, which runs the full width of the firebox, is also cast iron to reduce "hot spots" and to promote a longer burn.

The stove has a heat-resistant refractory bottom liner to insulate the stove bottom and to direct heat upwards.

Because preheated air produces better combustion, the insert is engineered to let cold air enter the stove through the air intake baffle (in the bell) and pass through a preheat chamber before it reaches the fire. There is also a secondary air inlet with an adjustable draft control.

On both sides of the insert are ⅛-inch steel plate heating chambers. Room air enters through openings at the front and bottom of the chamber. It then flows around Turbuair™ convectors that convert the radiant heat rays to heated air, which flows into the room from the top of the chamber.

The stove has a 17-by-18-inch cooking surface—ideal for times when a power failure occurs.

The fireplace closure panels come in four sizes matched to the width and height of your fireplace opening. Fireplace Insert Model 7901 requires an opening of 26 inches. At the top and sides, the panels should overlap the masonry by 2 inches.

Company: Liberty Bell Stove Works, Inc.
162 Reed Avenue
West Hartford, CT 06110

Specifications:

Heating capacity: 44,000 Btu/hr.
Height: 25 in.
Width: 22½ in.
Depth: 29 in.
Fuel: Wood
Log length: 23 in.
Length of burn: 12 hrs.
Weight: 370 lbs.
Color: Black
Safety testing: UL

Lopi Fireplace Insert FL

The fireplace insert of Lopi Energy Systems is a striking combination of elegance and utility. The firebox is made of $5/16$- and $1/4$-inch steel. The cast-iron door frames are inset with beautifully etched glass which has been tested to a constant 1400°F. and an intermittent 1800°F.

The door handles are coiled to moderate the heat. A third handle in the top of the unit opens and closes a combination damper/baffle system to increase heat output by decreasing the rate at which the gases exit.

Lopi Energy Systems offers a 5-year warranty on their fireplace insert "as a statement of our confidence in product quality."

Company: Lopi Energy Systems, Inc.
13233 N.E. 16th
Bellevue, WA 98005

Specifications:

Heating capacity: 1200–1500 sq. ft.
Height: 22⅜ in.
Width: 29¼ in.
Depth: 18½ in. (into fireplace)
Flue: 8 in.
Fuel: Wood
Log length: 22 in.
Length of burn: 10 hrs.
Weight: 480 lbs.
Color: Black, brown, blue
Safety testing: Stove Testing Laboratory, Portland, OR

Monarch Convert-A-Fireplace Model BCF36A

The Monarch Convert-A-Fireplace is available in all-antique brass or with a black front and an attractive brass trim. No tools or structural changes are necessary to install the fireplace insert.

The firebox is firebrick-lined and the whole unit factory-insulated for greater heat retention. Heat is conducted through the heavy steel walls of the firebox to the surrounding steel chamber on the sides, top and back walls. Air heated in this heavy steel chamber is forced through warm-air louvres above the bifold doors by two blowers located at the base of the insert. The 75 cfm blowers have an infinite solid state speed control.

Primary air is controlled manually from the front of the unit; if outside air is available, an outside air lever on the side of the unit is used. As air enters the combustion chamber, it washes over the four tempered glass doors to keep them clean and cool. Combustion control possible with the Monarch results in longer lasting fires,

more heat and reduced fuel consumption.

The insert is made of 12-guage steel, the grate and adjustable flue damper of cast iron. The flue damper interlocks with the glass doors so that they won't open until the damper is open.

A screen comes as standard equipment.

Company: Monarch Range and
Heater Div.
Malleable Iron Range Co.
715 No. Spring
Beaver Dam, WI 53916

Specifications:

Height: 29½ in.
Width: 48 in.
Depth: 20½ in.
Fuel: Wood or coal
Weight: 310 lbs.
Color: Black with brass trim or all
antique brass
Safety testing: UL

Moravian Fireplace Insert #202

The Quaker Stove Co., Inc. produces box, parlor and wood/coal stoves as well as the Moravian Fireplace Insert. The stoves have been designed by Cyril L. and Lenore Rennels, professional sculptors and metalsmiths, and are distinctive for their arched lines and rugged construction. The cast-iron doors and faceplate are especially rugged because of the tight gasket seal and adjustable door latch.

The Vycor glass door panels add visual pleasure. They also make the operation of the fire more efficient because the fire can be continually monitored without opening the doors. The glass can withstand temperatures higher than those generated by wood as well as possible thermal shock caused by splashes of snow or water.

The insert is made of ¼-inch plate steel and lined with firebrick to distribute the heat more evenly and to add thermal mass. The stove is also horizontally baffled with ⁵/₁₆-inch plate steel, which directs the gases to the front of the stove for secondary combustion.

The draft is controlled by the slide controls in the bottom of the doors.

Company: Quaker Stove Co., Inc.
200 W. 5th Street
Lansdale, PA 19446

Specifications:

Heating capacity: 27,000 Btu/hr.
Height: 23¾ in.
Width: 26 in.
Depth: 12½ in.
Fuel: Wood
Log length: 20 in.
Weight: 410 lbs.
Safety testing: UL

Morsø 2B

The Morsø 2B is a Danish cast-iron box stove that has been manufactured by the same company since 1853. Unlike steel stoves, stoves of cast iron take longer to heat up. On the other hand, they retain the heat better, providing steady radiant heat for comfortable room temperatures.

The Morsø stoves have been architect-designed. They combine quality, craftsmanship, durability and simple graceful lines. All Morsø stoves are freestanding, but Models 2B, 1B and 6B are especially well adapted for fireplace installations.

The Morsøs have tall graceful legs to make fireviewing and ash removal easier. The added height also increases air circulation around the stove. The Morsø 2B can only be top vented, and because the Morsø stands 28.7 inches to the top of the stovepipe collar, the manufacturer offers optional 6-inch legs for fireplace installations.

The Morsø 2B is available in a dull black, vitreous enamel (porcelain) finish which prevents rust, eliminates stove polishing and adds to the stove's handsome appearance. The bottom of the firebox is slightly rounded for added strength, and the side panels have a squirrel and oak leaf design for added beauty as well as increased radiating surface.

Standard items with the Morsø 2B include two lengths of 18 gauge stovepipe, an elbow, wall thimble, stove poker and enough insulation to seal the stovepipe at the thimble.

The smokepipe is designed to fit *inside* the exhaust collar on the stove. Liquid creosote condensing on the inside of the pipe will flow back into the stove and be burned. If installed outside the exhaust collar, the stovepipe allows creosote to leak out and run down the stove.

The Morsø is airtight. Air enters the firebox only through the spin draft control, then into an air circulator box on the firedoor.

Company: Southport Stoves
(Importer)
1180 Stratford Road
Stratford, CT 06457

Specifications:

Heating capacity: 2,200–4,800 cu. ft.
Height: 28 in.
Width: 13 in.
Depth: 27½ in.
Fuel: Wood
Length of burn: 8–12 hrs.
Weight: 124 lbs.
Color: Brown, black, grey enamel
or opaque porcelain

Mt. Chocorua

Energy Harvesters Corporation manufactures two handsome stoves in its New England foundry. Although the stoves are of the same size and shape, one design-in-relief is in a Colonial style, and the side panels of the second model feature a scenic view of Mt. Chocorua.

Both stoves can be top vented and still fit into a shallow fireplace, or with a conventional elbow and a run of pipe to the damper, they can be back vented to be installed in or in front of an existing fireplace.

The Mt. Chocorua stove vents into 5-inch flue pipe. The size is smaller than required for most stoves to reduce the amount of heat sent up the chimney. The flue exhaust collar on rear-vented installations brings the stovepipe *inside* the stove. As a result any creosote which runs down inside the pipe will run back into the stove where it will be burned.

Before the stove is used, the legs will have to be installed. There are three positions for the front legs depending on the depth of the front hearth.

The walls of the stove are of ¼-inch

cast iron. The inside of the firebox is baffled for greater heat output, and the draft openings are also baffled to prevent sparks from escaping. The firebox has interior ribs which hold the wood away from the sides. This design adds strength to the stove and allows better air circulation.

The deep hearth extension provides greater safety protection and helps prevent wood chips from falling to the floor while the stove is being loaded. The apron also results in less mess around the floor when removing the ashes.

The angled sides of the stove provide increased heat distribution, and the lift-out slate ash lip makes ash clean-up easier. To remove the slate, push through the finger hole beneath the slate. Clean off. Then sweep debris on the apron through the hole, catching the sweepings with the slate.

The 9¼-by-10-inch loading door will accept large, even twisted, logs with ease.

Company: Energy Harvesters Corp.
        Route 12, Box 19
        Fitzwilliam, NH 03447

Specifications:

    Heating capacity: 35,000 Btu/hr.
    Height: 26¾ in.
            27½ in. (to top exit)
    Width: 18½ in.
    Depth: 34½ in.
    Flue: 5 in.
    Fuel: Wood
    Log length: 18–20 in.
    Length of burn: 18 hrs.
    Weight: 225 lbs.
    Color: Black
    Safety testing: ETL of Maine

The Northwood Fireplace Insert

The Northwood Fireplace Insert easily slides into a fireplace opening, and once the edges are sealed with fiberglass, the insert is ready to use.

Solid brass accents on the doors and trim around the closure panel moderate the stark design of the insert.

The Northwood is double jacketed. The outside air jacket is made of ⅛-inch, the firebox of ¼-inch, the front plate and doors of ⅜-inch plate steel. This double-wall construction sets up a natural convection pattern of cool air entering below the firebox and heated air exiting above the fire doors. To increase heat output even further, the bottom, back and sides of the firebox are at angles to induce a larger volume of air through the insert. The design gives further momentum to the hot air.

The Northwood produces more heat in the home and less up the chimney. So that the fire is not cooled, both the primary and secondary air are pre-heated. The dual spin draft controls in the doors and the airtight construction of the insert give the operator total control over the burning process. This results in longer-lasting burns. The damper plate also slows exhaust gases, allowing them to burn more completely.

Company: Cadillac Stove Works, Inc.
8998 E. 34 Road
Cadillac, MI 49601

Specifications:

Height: 31 in. (front), 22 in. (back)
Width: 45¼ in. (front), 22 in.(back)
Depth: 20 in.
Flue: 8 in.
Fuel: Wood
Weight: 450 lbs.
Color: Black with solid brass
accents
Safety testing: UL

Ol' Hickory In-Fireplace Model

Ol' Hickory manufactures three inserts, a freestanding fireplace, and a stepped stove. The freestanding unit is easily adapted to be a fireplace insert.

The insert fits almost any fireplace opening and is installed using the existing fireplace chimney.

The ⅝-inch cast-iron door is asbestos-lined for a tight seal; the rest of the stove is of ¼-inch steel with a firebox of double wall construction.

The Ol'Hickory insert is designed to increase heat output. Interior baffles boost the stove's efficiency by directing and restricting the air flow. The airtight construction of the stove and the four, forced-air directional vents located at the top and bottom of the stove with two per side increase heat further.

Ol' Hickory stoves come with a limited guarantee for the lifetime of the original owner.

Company: Ol' Hickory™ Woodstoves
Box 8008
Greenville, SC 29604

Specifications:

Heating capacity: 2,000 sq. ft.
Height: 21¾ in.
Width: 28 in.
Depth: 15 in.
Fuel: Wood
Weight: 310 lbs.
Color: Black

O.M. 55BL

DeVault Fab has an extensive line of freestanding, airtight, wood- and coal-burning stoves. For one of their models they offer a kit to close off the space between the stove and fireplace.

Their stoves and inserts are made of ¼-inch welded steel plate with cast-iron doors and twin air locks for control of the draft. On the fireplace model there is an optional blower that forces hot air across the top of the stove into the room.

The insert has a large ash shelf and an 18½-by-11-inch door opening that takes 2-foot logs. The firebrick lining increases heat retention and extends the life of the insert.

For safety and efficiency, all models have a tapered latch and rope seal to provide positive locking of the fire-doors. There are optional chrome accessories such as vent caps, handles, hinge pins and highlighted doors, which add a distinctive touch.

Fire screens are also an available accessory for all Old Mill stoves.

The stoves have a 25-year limited warranty and are reasonably priced "for the working man's pocketbook."

Company: DeVault Fab-Weld & Piping Co.
304 Old Mill Lane
Clover Hill Business Park
Exton, PA 19341

Specifications:

Heating capacity: 2200–2500 sq. ft.
Height: 22¼ in.
Width: 25 in.
Depth: 28 in.
Flue: 8 in.
Fuel: Wood
Log length: 22–24 in.
Length of burn: 8–10 hrs.
Weight: 454 lbs.
Color: Flat black
Safety testing: Arnold Greene Testing Labs

The Optima

Thermograte combines good-quality glass doors with an effective heat exchanger as a solution to fireplace inefficiency.

Conventional glass doors, recommended for open fireplaces as a heat-conserving measure, do not increase heat gain from a fireplace. They do prevent loss of warm room air, but without a heat exchanger, glass doors actually *reduce* the heat output of a fireplace unless the doors are left open while a fire is going. With its combination of glass doors and heat exchanger, the Optima reduces by 85 percent the heat normally lost up the chimney from a conventional fireplace and delivers 20,000–50,000 Btu/hr.

On the smaller models of the Optima there are six heat exchange tubes, eight on the larger models. Depending on the model, the tubes range from 22 to 27 inches in height and are fully welded. They are made of chrome-nickel stainless steel to insure longer

life. Because the tubes are highly oxidation-resistant means Thermograte can offer a 15-year warranty.

The large 1.9-inch diameter, 16-gauge stainless steel tubes deliver high heat output even without the blowers because the tubes create a large surface area with exposure in the hottest region of the fire.

The two whisper-quiet blowers have an infinitely variable speed control, and to improve the appearance of the unit they are concealed. The blowers deliver 150 cfm and use less power than a 100-watt bulb.

The insert has been designed to work by natural convection as well. When the blowers are off, the air drawn into the unit by natural convection is enough to keep the blowers from overheating. Without operating the blowers, heat output of up to 40,000 Btu/hr. is possible, which means that in a power blackout the unit will still function.

The ¼-inch, picture-window, bifold, tempered glass doors are designed not to get dirty; moving air around the doors keeps the glass clean and cool. However, should the doors need cleaning they are easily removed.

Company: Thermograte, Inc.
2785 N. Fairview Avenue
St. Paul, MN 55113

Specifications:

Heating capacity: 20,000–50,000 Btu/hr.
Height: 18½ in.
Depth: 17 in. (bottom), 14½ in. (top)
Safety testing: UL

Phoenix Fireplace Insert™ 4880

The Phoenix Fireplace Insert™ 4880 is built for rugged use. Hinge uprights, knobs, slides, glass panels and flanges all bolt to the unit for easy adjustment and/or replacement. An entire door can be lifted out whenever the glass panels need cleaning. Should a panel break, a second panel is easily secured in place with no more than a wrench and screwdriver.

The insert is also easy to install. Simply slide it in to the desired depth. (The fireplace opening must be 33 to 56 inches wide.) The adjustable flanges should fit snugly against marble, tile, brick, stone or any other fireplace facing, and the unit can be as easily removed for chimney cleaning.

The Phoenix is of double-wall, steel construction. Cold air is drawn in under the firebox. It moves by natural convection up the back and over the top of the firebox; the heated air is then vented into the room.

An optional, variable speed, transflow blower will greatly increase the convected draft pattern.

Company: Phoenix Manufacturing Corp.
P.O. Box 2637
Asheville, NC 28802

Specifications:

Heating capacity: 2,000 sq. ft.
Height: 23⅝ in.
Width: 32⅜ in.
Depth: 22 in.
Fuel: Wood or coal
Log length: 30 in.
Length of burn: 8–10 hrs.
Weight: 417 lbs.
Color: Black
Safety testing: AGTL

Pine Barren Coal-Wood Fireplace Insert

The Pine Barren Coal-Wood Fireplace Insert burns either wood or coal and slips into a fireplace opening 28 to 44 inches wide and 23⅞ to 33 inches high.

The firebox has a double-walled heat exchanger and is firebrick lined. Two thermostatically controlled fans fit into the sides of the insert so as to be invisible. The fans have variable-speed controls so that you can regulate the blower to suit your needs.

A cast-iron rotating shaker grate with an external, easy-to-use lever allows you to shake the grates with a minimum of dust and ash. A sturdy pull-out ash pan is conveniently located.

The high-strength, tempered glass window lets you enjoy the fire, and the secondary air inlet directs a flow of air along the firedoor window to keep it clean and cool. There is also a fully adjustable primary air control and a secondary air inlet for more effective burning of the volatile gases.

The stove is available in a black finish with handsome brass trim. There is an optional brass hood that is decorative and protects a wooden mantel or nearby combustibles.

Company: Pine Barren International
P.O. Box 494, Route 72
Chatsworth, NJ 08019

Specifications:

Heating capacity: 2,000 sq. ft.
Height: 23⅞ in.
Width: 28 in.
Depth: 20½ in.
Fuel: Wood or coal
Log length: 18½ in.
Length of burn: 18 hrs. (wood),
30 hrs. (coal)
Weight: 410 lbs.
Color: Black with brass trim
Safety testing: ETL Testing
Laboratories

Resolute Woodstove

Vermont Castings has been continually expanding its well-known line of cast-iron stoves. The company offers three wood-burning models: the Vigilant, the Defiant and the Resolute; and two coal-burning models: the Vigilant Coal Stove and the Resolute Coal Stove. They also offer a reversible flue collar for top or rear venting and cast-iron or glass doors.

All models are inspired by the design, engineering principles and construction of Vermont Castings' first stove, the Defiant. The arched detailing of the front loading doors and the fluted cook top are reminiscent of the late eighteenth century American Franklin-type stove, and are an aesthetic addition to any home.

The low flue collar height of the Resolute, the smallest of the stoves, makes it ideal for installation in almost any fireplace.

The stove can be loaded from the front or top with a top loading door of 12⅞ by 7⅛ inches and a front door opening of 13⅝ by 11⅝ inches.

All Vermont Castings models are engineered for maximum burning efficiency. The thermostat automatically controls the air intake. Incoming oxygen is dispersed around the sides and back of the stove to allow the air to be pre-heated before it enters the combustion zone. This decreases the amount of wood consumed. The air then enters the firebox at the bottom of the wood load through air entry ports.

The manual secondary air control allows the volatiles to escape into the secondary combustion chamber through the secondary air tube. In the secondary combustion chamber the unburned gases combine with oxygen to provide additional heat before they pass behind the internal baffle and out the flue.

An internal damper, when lowered, permits the stove to be used as a fireplace. When raised, it helps increase heating efficiency.

Company: Vermont Castings Inc.
　　　　　Prince Street
　　　　　Randolph, VT 05060

Specifications:

Heating capacity: 35,000 Btu/hr.
Height: 26 in.
Width: 26¼ in.
Depth: 17 in.
Flue: 6 in.
Fuel: Wood (coal convertible)
Log length: 16 in.
Length of burn: 8–10 hrs.
Weight: 253 lbs.
Color: Black
Safety testing: Arnold Greene
　　　　　　　Testing Labs

Russo Coal/Wood Combo

The Russo is a coal/wood combination stove, but to burn coal you will need the optional coal basket and shaker grates. The unit features an internal heat exchanger and baffle. The glass window in the front loading door radiates heat while you enjoy the fire.

The stove has a built-in damper and front ash drawer. Because the stove is only 26½ inches high it will fit into or in front of most fireplace openings.

A thermostatically-controlled blower is available should you wish to increase the rate of convected air from the stove.

Russo combination stoves are constructed of heavy, ³/₁₆-inch and 10-gauge plate steel.

The extra large, front-loading door, the flue damper and air intake make long burn times easy.

Company: Russo Manufacturing Corp.
87 Warren Street
Randolph, MA 02368

Specifications:

Heating capacity: 14,000 cu. ft.
Height: 26½ in.
Width: 25⅛ in.
Depth: 17 in. (plus an additional
10 in. for blower)
Flue: 6 in.
Fuel: Coal or wood
Log length: 18 in.
Length of burn: 10 hrs. (wood),
28 hrs. (coal)
Weight: 325 lbs.
Color: Different colors available
Safety testing: Arnold Greene
Testing Labs

The Shelburne Fireplace Stove

The Shelburne is efficient, safe and well designed. The stove is of double-wall, steel and cast iron construction and is fitted with four rugged wheels. The wheels allow one person to roll the 550-pound unit in and out of the fireplace for periodic cleaning of the baffle system and chimney. Three cast iron flanges seal the unit against the fireplace opening.

The optional transparent Corning Pyroceram glass firedoors are shatter resistant as well as being good conductors of heat. They will not crack or explode from high heat or impact. You can keep an eye on the fire and make draft adjustments without having to open the doors. The handle at the front of the insert adjusts the automatic thermostat.

The 160-cfm blower is located at the rear of the unit and is easily accessible once the unit is rolled out of the fireplace opening. The blower speed control can be located on the wall near by.

Once switched on, the blower accelerates the natural convection cycle by drawing cool air in through the ducts behind the lower grille. The air travels from the intake ducts along the back of the unit through the air plenum and is exhausted out the twin ducts behind the brass grille.

Company: The Vermont Stove Co.
Route 7, Shelburne Road
Shelburne, VT 05482

Specifications:

Heating capacity: 24,000–30,000
Btu/hr.
Height: 25¾ in.
Width: 26 in.
Depth: 17 in. (extends 16 in. into
fireplace)
Fuel: Wood
Log length: 20 in.
Length of burn: 8 hrs.
Weight: 550 lbs.
Color: Black with brass grilles

Shenandoah FP-I

The blowers have a manual and an automatic thermostat switch. When set on automatic, they operate whenever sufficient heat exists in the firebox. Other features of the stove include a firebrick lining for greater heat retention and an ash pan for easy ash removel.

The insert can be used in the firebox mode if the gasketed glass doors are left open and a firescreen is used to prevent sparks from flying out of the aluminized firebox.

The insert will fit fireplace openings ranging from 30 to 40 inches in width and 25 to 30 inches in height. The unit can be fully inserted or extend 8 inches onto the hearth; only a minimal fireplace depth of 14 inches is required.

Shenandoah Manufacturing offers 13 durable models of wood- and coal-burning stoves. Many are versatile. The Shenandoah Fireplace Insert, for example, may be either a fireplace insert or a freestanding circulating heater. As an insert, the unit comes with an enclosure shield; as a freestanding unit, the stove comes with a set of legs.

The fireplace unit is installed easily and comes with a cast-iron grate for burning wood or coal. A bi-metallic thermostat controls the rate of burn; inlets provide primary and secondary air as needed.

At the bottom and to either side of the insert are two variable-speed fans. They draw in cool room air. To extract heat from the firebox, they force the air through the baffled, double-walled heat chamber. The heat travels behind and over the firebox; it is then discharged through vents above the loading doors.

Company: Shenandoah Mfg.
Co.,Inc.
P.O. Box 839
Harrisonburg, VA 22801

Specifications:

Height: 25 in.
Width: 26 in.
Depth: 20 in.
Flue: 8 in.
Fuel: Wood or coal
Weight: 400 lbs.
Color: Black
Safety testing: ETL of Maine

Super Heat Fireplace Insert

The Super Heat Fireplace Insert is adaptable to almost any fireplace opening. The standard model will fit if the fireplace opening is 13½ inches deep; the opening must be 26–38 inches wide at the bottom and 23¼–29 inches wide at the top. Perfection Manufacturing also offers a Super Heat Extender Kit which adapts the unit to openings up to 50 inches wide by 32 inches high. Extra side panels snap on, and a 3-inch top panel, which includes a heat deflector, increases the height.

There are further options. To make the front of the unit more aesthetically pleasing, ceramic tiles can be added around the airtight firedoor. The colors for the tiles include gloss black, barn red, hearth brown, burnt orange, and antique white.

The Super Heat Fireplace Insert is fiberglass insulated. The walls are double. Two 75-cfm whisper fans at either side of the unit draw cool air in the inlets and circulate it through channels between the firebox and the outer wall. As the air is heated it rises along the back wall and over the top of the unit, reaching the room through outlets in the top of the unit or through vents in the canopy.

The Super Heat carries most of the heated air into your house because the insert has only 48 square inches of exhaust flue. Normal fireplaces have damper openings from 96 to 120 square inches; therefore the draft of the fire pulls most of the heat up the chimney.

The insert sets 13½ inches into the fireplace with 10 inches of the unit resting on the hearth. This further increases the amount of radiated heat. And the three-panel Corning, high-temperature Pyroceram^R glass transmits heat while allowing a view of the fire.

At the rear of the firebox, leveling shoes can be adjusted within a 2-inch range if the fireplace floor is uneven.

Company: KNT Division
Perfection Mfg. Corp.
P.O. Box 1365
Mansfield, OH 44901

Specifications:

Heating capacity: 38,850 Btu/hr.
Height: 29 in. (front),
23½ in. (back)
Width: 38 in. (front),
26 in. (back)
Depth: 23½ in. (13½ in. into
fireplace opening,
10 in. onto hearth)
Fuel: Wood or coal
Log length: 18 in.
Length of burn: 8 hrs.
Weight: 290 lbs.
Color: Black with optional front
ceramic tiles
Safety testing: Arnold Greene
Testing Labs

Thor Fireplace Insert

Thor Metal Works Ltd. offers wood and coal/wood fireplace inserts. With the company's products comes an owner's manual with general information, detailed installation instructions, operating procedures and emergency measures.

Before the insert is installed, the fireplace damper must be locked in an open position. A length of stainless steel pipe to direct the gases up the chimney is then pushed into the damper opening. Once the insert is slid into the fireplace, the smokepipe is pulled back down to attach to the flue collar on the insert.

Shrouds for blocking off the fireplace come in three sizes: standard, medium and extra large, and they can be mounted anywhere on the fireplace insert. This allows you to position the insert at any convenient depth into the fireplace.

The standard stove-black shroud is screwed together. If the optional canopy hood is purchased, it fits behind the top of the shroud. The canopy provides protection for wood mantels and comes in an attractive antique brass finish.

The three shroud sizes and the tapered rear of the stove mean the unit should fit 95 percent of the fireplace openings.

A blower/ash fender assembly is standard. It is installed in front of the stove. No special tools are necessary. The blower package is inserted into a slot under the door; a speed control is optional.

Because the stove is of double-wall construction, the fan draws cooler air through the lower opening into the outer chamber and releases warm air at the top of the insert.

The airtight, ¼-inch plate steel firebox must be lined along the bottom and sides with firebrick. The firebrick comes with the unit along with steel retainer bars to hold the upright bricks in place. The fire is laid directly on top of the firebrick.

The stove features double-pane glass. The inner pane is highly resistant to heat shock; the outer is ¼-inch, impact-resistant glass.

Company: Thor Metal Works, Ltd.
P.O. Box 378
Eastwood Station
Syracuse, NY 13206

Specifications:

Heating capacity: 2,400 sq. ft.
Height: 24¼ in.
Width: 27 in.
Depth: 20½ in.
Flue: 8 in.
Fuel: Wood
Log length: 20 in.
Length of burn: 6–8 hrs.
Weight: 500 lbs. (s.w.)
Color: Black
Safety testing: UL

Timberline Fireplace Insert TP-FI

The Timberline Fireplace Insert is made of steel plate construction with interlocking cast-iron doors.

Air for combustion is regulated by knob draft controls on the front loading doors. Because of the double-wall construction, air also circulates in a chamber under, behind and over the firebox. Cool air is drawn in from the room by natural convection; heated air is released, thereby maximizing heating efficiency. This outer shell of air, by decreasing the radiant heat loss through the insert walls, keeps most of the heat inside the unit.

The baffle inside the firebox and the firebrick lining increase heat retention. The firebrick also protects the unit from warping.

The Timberline is readily installed into an existing fireplace.

The insert comes with a 5-year limited warranty and is not recommended for zero-clearance fireplaces.

Company: Timberline International, Inc.
P.O. Box 4307
Boise, ID 83704

Specifications:

Heating capacity: 1,700 sq. ft.
Height: 21 in.
Width: 26 in.
Depth: 14½ in. (extending into fireplace)
Fuel: Wood
Log length: 20 in.
Weight: 530 lbs.
Color: Black
Safety testing: UL

Upland #207

The Upland Model #207 is a free-standing, combination airtight and fireplace woodstove with attractive, classical lines. The option of top or rear venting means the stove can be easily installed for use as a fireplace insert. The stove is constructed of ¼-inch cast iron to insure that the stove won't warp or lose its airtightness.

The stove requires minimal assembly. Bolt the four 7-inch legs to the stove and insert the two heat baffles which should rest on shelves in the firebox.

By adjusting the baffles, the Upland can be burned in the fireplace or airtight mode.

When the stove is used as a fireplace, open the side fire-door and move the baffle nearest the front loading door closer to the side-loading door. This adjustment will more directly vent the hot gases. Build the fire near the rear of the stove. Leave the front-loading doors open, but be sure the spark screen is securely in place. Once the fire is burning well the damper can be adjusted without forcing smoke into the room.

When the stove is used in the airtight mode, the baffles must be placed side by side so that they touch each other. Start the fire near the side fire-door.

In the airtight mode the wood burns from left to right (or front to back) which establishes an "S" pattern of gases through the firebox. When the gases reach the fresh air vent they ignite. This controlled-burn pattern increases the heat output of the stove and minimizes creosote build-up.

The mode of operation can be changed while the fire is burning. The Upland will burn 24 hours on two loads of seasoned wood.

As standard items the unit includes a fire screen and a 28-inch ash hoe, as well as a door opening tool for when the handles and controls are too hot to touch.

The stove comes with a 1-year full guarantee and is not for use in mobile homes.

Company: Upland Stove Co., Inc.
Box 338, 2 Green Street
Greene, NY 13778

Specifications:
Heating capacity: 50,000 Btu/hr.
Height: 30 in.
Width: 32 in.
Depth: 18.5 in.
Flue: 7 in.
Fuel: Wood
Log length: 26 in.
Length of burn: 10 hrs.
Weight: 300 lbs.
Color: Black
Safety testing: ETL of Maine

The Villager

The Villager stove was designed for visual appeal, convenience and efficiency. The stove face incorporates traditional styling and a Pyrex glass window for fire viewing. The stove's air control knobs are white porcelain; they remain cool to the touch.

Many stoves can be vented into an existing fireplace as long as the distance to the top of the flue collar is less than the height of the fireplace. The Villager is 24½ inches to the flue top, and it should fit most fireplace openings.

The unit, which burns either wood or coal, is constructed of ¼-inch and ⁵/₁₆-inch boiler plate steel. The doors are heavy cast iron, as is the coal shaker-grate system. The combustion chamber is lined with firebrick.

There's a large door for loading fuel, and a separate lower door and ash drawer for removing ashes. An ash fender helps protect flooring and makes ash removal safer.

Another feature of this stove is the heat extractor designed to enhance efficiency. A cross-flow, secondary-air induction system promotes combustion of volatile gases. And an optional blower system also improves the unit's performance.

The manufacturer says the Villager can produce up to 86,000 Btu per hour for a six hour period on a single load of fuel. The stove holds 60 pounds of coal or 16-inch firelogs.

The Villager has a 23-by-16-inch cook top, which can add to the stove's versatility.

The stove was tested to U.L. standard 1482 by R.F. Geisser and Associates.

The Villager is guaranteed to be free of manufacturing (workmanship) defects for a period of five years from the date of purchase by the original owner, with the following exceptions: cast-iron grate system, gaskets, glass, firebricks and paint.

Company: Hicks-Millar Company
Main Street
Bradford, NH 03221

Specifications:

Heating capacity: 16,000 cu. ft.
Height: 26 in.
Width: 23¼ in.
Depth: 23 in. (includes heat
   extractor)
Flue: 6 in.
Fuel: Wood or coal
Log length: 16 in.
Length of burn: 10–20 hrs.
Weight: 310 lbs.
Color: Black
Safety testing: R.F. Geisser
   and Associates

Welenco FHE 36

The Welenco FHE 36 is designed to increase the efficiency of the 36-inch-wide Standex Energy Systems Woodside W36 and W36 Zero-Clearance Fireplaces.

The Welenco is a tubular heat exchanger with a built-in, twin fan blower. The heat exchange tubes increase heat and decrease the wood consumption of a conventional fireplace. They also prevent the creosote buildup experienced with most airtight woodstoves.

The unit is made of $^3/_{16}$-inch steel with brass trim on the door and base. Standard items include a fire screen and a hinged $^3/_{16}$-inch tempered glass door for fireviewing.

With the outside air combination unit, the Welenco is approved for use in mobile and modular housing.

Company: Welenco Mfg. Inc.
1545 7th Ave. North
Lewiston, ID 83501

Specifications:

Heating capacity: 83,400 Btu/hr.
Height: 27 in.
Width: 34 in.
Depth: 17 in.
Fuel: Wood or coal
Log length: 28 in.
Length of burn: 6–8 hrs.
Weight: 200 lbs.
Color: Black
Safety testing: Warnock Hersey Ltd.

Woodland Fireplace Insert FI-25

Woodland manufactures nine different models including freestanding stoves, freestanding fireplaces, and fireplace inserts. Because all Woodland stoves are available with top or rear exhaust, they are easily vented into a fireplace opening. The Woodland FI-25 Fireplace Insert fits a fireplace opening up to 40 inches wide; flashing kits are available for larger sized openings.

The overall depth of the FI-25 is 36 inches, 16 inches of this extends out from the fireplace opening. If you can afford the space, there are many advantages to this design. Radiant heat is distributed in all directions; rising heat hits a metal mantle deflector and is directed into the room. The insert also produces convected heat. There is space to allow air to travel under, then over, the stove to re-enter the room as heated air.

The FI-25 is made of ¼-inch (sides and bottom) and ⁵/₁₆-inch (top) steel plate. The firebox is airtight and lined with 28 firebricks to prevent burnout. Heavy-duty cast-iron doors are gasket sealed, and the coil-type door handles remain cool to the touch.

The unit can be burned with the doors open for the full enjoyment of watching the fire; a firescreen is standard equipment for all Woodland models of double door construction. Other features include a large ash apron, manual draft caps mounted in the firedoors and a large 11- by 17-inch opening to take awkward logs. Built into the flue outlet is the control handle for the damper which is accessible from the front of the unit. The nickel-plated trim around the closure panels adds a classic elegance to the Insert.

Woodland offers a choice of cast-iron or Vycor^R thermal glass fire doors; the blower unit, however, is optional.

Woodland stoves are designed to burn wood or bituminous coal; they are not designed for use with factory-built or zero-clearance fireplaces.

Company: Woodland Stoves
of America
1460 W. Airline Hwy.
Waterloo, IA 50703

Specifications:

Heating capacity: 2500 sq. ft.
Height: 23 in.
Width: 35½ in.
Depth: 20 in. inside fireplace,
16 in. outside
Flue: 8 in.
Fuel: Wood or coal
Log length: 27 in.
Length of burn: 10–14 hrs.
Weight: 585 lbs.
Color: Black
Safety testing: Northwest
Laboratories

FP6-79U Woodmaster Fireplace Insert

Suburban has two new decorator-designed fireplace inserts — the Woodmaster and the Woodmaster/Coalmaster Deluxe Fireplace Insert. The latter has dual fuel capability and a built-in humidifier to solve the problem of winter-dry rooms.

Both models feature a thermostatically controlled blower that automatically draws cool air from the room, circulates it through the unit, then returns heated air back into the room. Decorative brass fittings, double-door construction and a generous fireviewing area are standard items. For cleaning convenience, there is a removable ash pan with handle.

The Woodmaster insert fits most conventional fireplaces.

Suburban also manufactures a wood-burning circulator for mobile homes, freestanding stoves and an add-on wood furnace.

Company: Suburban Manufacturing Co.
P.O. Box 399
Dayton, TN 37321

Specifications:

Heating capacity: Up to 50,000 Btu/hr.
Height: 32½ in.
Width: 44 in.
Depth: 20 in.
Fuel: Wood
Log length: 22 in.
Length of burn: 5–8 hrs.
Weight: 250 lbs.
Color: Black with brass trim
Safety testing: UL

References

Books

Bartok, John W. Jr. *Heating With Coal*. Charlotte, Vermont: Garden Way Publishing Co., 1980.

Curtis, Christopher, and Post, Donald. *Be Your Own Chimney Sweep*. Charlotte, Vermont: Garden Way Publishing Co., 1979.

Eastman, Margaret and Wilbur F. Jr. *Planning and Building Your Fireplace*. Charlotte, Vermont: Garden Way Publishing Co., 1976.

Gay, Larry. *The Complete Book of Heating With Wood*. Charlotte, Vermont: Garden Way Publishing Co., 1974.

Kern, Ken and Magers, Steve. *Fireplaces: The Owner-Builder's Guide*. New York: Charles Scribner's Sons, 1978.

Lytle, R.J. and M.J. *Book of Successful Fireplaces*, Farmington, Michigan: Structures Publishing, 1977.

Mercer, Henry C. *The Bible in Iron*. Narberth, Pennsylvania: Livingston Publishing Co., 1961.

Orton, Vrest. *The Forgotten Art of Building a Good Fireplace*. Dublin, New Hampshire: Yankee Books, 1969.

Rowsome, Frank. *A Bright and Glowing Place*. Brattleboro, Vermont: Stephen Greene Press, 1975.

Shelton, Jay W. *The Woodburner's Encyclopedia*. Waitsfield, Vermont: Crossroads Press, 1976.

Shelton, Jay W. *Wood Heat Safety*. Charlotte, Vermont: Garden Way Publishing Co., 1979.

Sparks, Jared, ed. *The Works of Benjamin Franklin*. Chicago: Townsend MacCoun, 1882.

Sparrow, W.J. *Count Rumford of Woburn, Massachusetts*. New York: Thomas Y. Crowell Co., 1964.

Twitchell, Mary. *Wood Energy: A Practical Guide To Heating With Wood*. Charlotte, Vermont: Garden Way Publishing Co., 1978.

Articles, Bulletins, Reports

American Society of Heating, Air-Conditioning and Refrigerating Engineers. *ASHRAE Handbook of Fundamentals*, Chapter 26. New York, 1973.

Bear, David. "The World's Heaviest Woodstove." *Rodale's New Shelter*, January 1981.

Busch, Robert D., and Ireland, Richard, "Analysis of Heat-Saving Retrofit Devices For Fireplaces." New Mexico Energy Institute, University of New Mexico, March 1979.

Edwards, Harrison. "The Norwich Laboratory Report on Fireplaces." Norwich, New York, 1977.

"Fireplace Energy Savers." *Consumer Reports*, January 1981.

Gaynor, John. "How to Keep the Home Fires Burning Safely." *Popular Mechanics*, October 1980.

Kristia Associates. "Jotul: A Resource Book On The Art Of Heating With Wood." Kristia Associates, Portland, Maine, 1973.

Langa, F.S. "Wood As Fuel: How To Calculate The Economics." *Popular Science*, February 1978.

Manley, Patrick J. "The Ins and Outs of A Wonderfully Efficient Wood-burning System." *Farmstead Magazine*, Fall 1980.

Modera, M.P. and Sonderegger, R.C. "Determination of In-Situ Performance of Fireplaces." Lawrence Berkeley Laboratory, University of California, August 1980.

Roberts, Louis O. "Masonry Fireplace Stove" (plans). Timeless Products, Roxbury, Connecticut, 1977.

Shelton, Jay W. "Measured Performance of Fireplaces and Fireplace Accessories." Shelton Energy Research,

P.O. Box 5235 Coronado Station, Santa Fe, New Mexico, 87502, 1978.

Shelton, et al. "Woodstove Testing Methods and Some Preliminary Experimental Results." ASHRAE Transactions, Vol. 48, Part 1, 1978.

Stone, R.L. "Fireplace Operation Depends on Good Chimney Design." *ASHRAE Journal*, February 1969.

Trefil, James. "Fireplace Efficiency Boosters — How Do They Rate?" *Popular Science*, November 1979.

Underwriter's Laboratories. UL737, UL 1482, safety standards for Fireplace Stoves and Solid-Fuel-Type Room Heaters, Underwriter's Laboratories, Inc., 333 Pfingsten Road, Northbrook, Ill. 60062.

University of Illinois. "Fuel Savings Resulting From Closing of Rooms and From Use of a Fireplace." Bulletin, Vol. 41, No. 13, November 1943.

United States Department of Agriculture. "Fireplaces and Chimneys." Farmer's Bulletin No. 1889, USDA, Washington, D.C., 1941.

Zimmerman, Mark D. "Energy Options for the '80s: Rekindling an Interest in Wood." *Machine Design Magazine*, January 22, 1981.

Glossary

Anthracite
A hard coal having very little dust, smoke or volatiles. It contains more than 90 percent carbon and is more difficult to ignite than other types of coal.

Approved
A stove that has been accepted for installation by the state or local building official or fire marshal.

Asbestos millboard
Soft asbestos board used as a non-combustible material. Because of potential health damage from breathing the asbestos fibers, mouth protection should be used when cutting this material.

Ash
The unburnable mineral part of coal or wood. The amounts in different types of coal or wood vary widely.

Ash dump
The metal opening in the floor of the hearth through which ashes are raked into the ash pit below.

Ash pit
The storage area in the bottom of a chimney where ashes are accumulated under the hearth.

Back hearth
The floor of the fire chamber where the fire is laid.

Bituminous coal
A soft coal having considerable volatile matter which is given off as a smoky gas when heated. It is high in heat value.

Breast
That part of the front of the fireplace between the lintel and the throat.

Briquettes
Molded blocks or pellets of coal dust available in bag quantities.

Btu (British thermal unit)
The amount of energy required to raise a pound of water 1° Fahrenheit. One thousand Btu will heat one gallon of water 120° F.

Cannel coal
A noncaking coal that contains trapped oil. It burns with a bright, hot flame. It should not be used in closed stoves.

Chimney cap
This refers to protective metal or masonry tops for chimneys.

Clinker
A lump of melted ash that forms when hot coals mix with the ash layer. Clinkers should be removed so they don't block the grate or inhibit combustion.

Combination unit
A fireplace heating unit that combines a tubular grate with glass doors.

Conduction
The transfer of heat through an object or surface.

Convection
The transfer of heat through natural or forced circulation.

Covings
The right and left sides of the fire chamber.

Cleanout Door
The door at the base of a chimney used to clean out soot, ash and creosote.

Collar (or flue collar)
The part of a fuel-burning appliance to which the chimney connector or chimney attaches.

Creosote
Chimney and stovepipe deposits originating as condensed wood

smoke (including vapors, tar and soot). Creosote is often initially liquid, but may dry to a flaky or solid form.

Damper
A device inserted in a chimney or chimney connector or stove to control the draft on the fire.

Elbow
Stovepipe fittings or sections involving turns or bends. 90-degree elbows are most common.

Energy efficiency
The percentage of the total energy content of the fuel consumed that becomes useful heat in the house.

Facing
A layer of non-combustible material around the top and sides of the fireplace opening.

Factory-built chimney
A double-wall insulated or triple-wall approved chimney. It is often less expensive to install than a masonry chimney.

Fireback
The rear wall of the fire chamber. Usually pertains to the vertical section of the rear wall, while the slanted section is the *slope of fireback*. Also refers to a heavy, cast-iron plate used to protect masonry and to enhance reflection of radiant heat from a fireplace.

Firebox
The chamber of a stove or fireplace where the fire burns.

Firebrick
Brick capable of withstanding high temperatures, such as in stoves, furnaces and boilers. Different types of firebrick have different temperature limits.

Fireclay
Clay that will withstand high temperatures without cracking or deforming. NFPA recommends that fireclay chimney flue liners resist

corrosion, softening or cracking from flue gases at temperatures up to 1800° F.

Fireplace furnace
A factory-built or zero-clearance fireplace designed as a system for heating an entire home.

Fireplace opening
The opening into the fire chamber where fuel is burned.

Fireplace stove
A free-standing, solid-fuel-burning, room-heating appliance operated either with its fire chamber open or closed.

Flashing
Metal pieces used to form a barrier to prevent moisture from leaking between the chimney and the roof or other woodwork.

Flue
A passage in the chimney for smoke and gases to escape.

Flue liner
A hollow length of vitrified fireclay made to line the inside of flues.

Frame
Usually a border of wood or metal around the outer edges of the fireplace facing.

Front hearth
The extension of the back hearth into the room to provide protection against sparks from the fireplaces.

Grate
A framework of iron bars that support the fire and allow combustion air to pass through. Generally cast iron is used.

Hearth
The floor of the fire chamber where the fire is built. It also includes the front hearth although the word "hearth" frequently refers only to the back hearth.

Heat reclaimer
A stovepipe device to recover heat that would normally be lost.

Insert
A room-heating appliance that fits within the opening of a conventional fireplace. It is usually of double-wall construction so that additional heat can be gained from the fire and circulated within the room.

Jambs
The front sides of the fireplace opening.

Lintel
A plate of steel or stone across the top of the fireplace opening to support masonry.

Listed
A stove model that has passed a comprehensive safety test by an accepted testing laboratory. Some states require that all new stoves sold be listed.

Mantel
A sort of shelf above the fireplace, frequently used to hold decorative articles such as candles and clocks. It may also be part of the frame.

Night cover
A cover of metal or some other noncombustible material placed over the fireplace opening to prevent warm room air from escaping up the flue. Most often used at night or during a waning fire.

NFPA
The National Fire Protection Association, 470 Atlantic Avenue, Boston, MA 02210. An independent, not-for-profit organization for fire safety. Many jurisdictions adopt NFPA standards as part of their codes.

Peat
The product of partial decay of plants that accumulate in stagnant water in swamps and lakes. It is used as a fuel in some countries.

Primary air
Air for combustion that enters the stove below the grate. This air supply controls the intensity of the fire.

Radiation
The emission of infrared rays of energy that heat whatever surfaces are immediately in line with the heat source, the fire.

Russian fireplace
A massive, masonry fireplace that retains heat long after a fire has been left to wane. Features an intricate, interior baffle system and efficient combustion.

Secondary air
Air for combustion that enters the stove above the level of the fire. This air supplies the oxygen to help burn the volatile gases.

Slope of fireback
The slanted section of the fireback.

Smoke chamber
That area above the throat which is reduced in size as it is built upward until it reaches the flue.

Smoke shelf
The horizontal shelf above, and running the length of, the throat. It turns the down-drafts around to prevent them from forcing smoke into the room via the fire chamber.

Soot
A carbon substance that results from incomplete combustion and is deposited inside the stovepipe and chimney.

Spark arrester
A mesh cap on top of the flue to prevent sparks from being carried outside by the updrafts and to prevent birds and animals from entering the flue.

Thimble
A metal or clay connector that supports stovepipe as it passes through a wall.

Throat
An opening 3 or 4 inches wide running the length of the fire chamber where the breast and slope of fireback otherwise would meet. Smoke and gases from the fire must pass through the throat to get into the

flue. The damper rests over the throat.

Tube grates
A fireplace grate with a series of tubes, often C-shaped. Cool air enters the base of the tubes, then, after warming from the fire, convects back into the room.

Volatiles
The vapors, mostly hydrocarbons, that are driven off when a fuel is burned.

Zero clearance fireplace
A factory-built metal fireplace with multi-layer construction providing enough insulation and/or air cooling so that the base, back, and in some cases sides, can safely be placed in direct contact ("zero clearance") with combustible floors and walls.

Acknowledgements

Many people contributed significantly to this book project: Bob Bennett and Kathy Smith of Garden Way offered early encouragement and assistance; Bob Vogel drew excellent illustrations; Sandy Goddard typed the manuscript quickly and accurately; Fred Stetson edited it; and, most importantly, my wife, Kate, gave generous and much-appreciated support and feedback.

Several technical experts and organizations also provided valuable assistance or published influential and helpful studies: John Bartok, author of *Heating With Coal*; Chris Curtis and Don Post of Black Magic Chimney Sweeps; A.C.S. "Skip" Hayden of the Canadian Combustion Research Laboratory; Charles Page of Vermont Castings; Larry Scanlon of The Burning Log stove store; Jay W. Shelton, director of Shelton Energy Research; Mary Twitchell, author of *Wood Energy*; Albert Ulmer of Williston, Vermont; The Shelburne Museum; Underwriter's Laboratory; the University of Vermont Bailey Library; and the Wood Heating Alliance.

Finally, I'd like to thank all the manufacturers who furnished product information and photographs. Especially noteworthy are those who not only developed quality products, but tested them for safety and efficiency, and then made their test results available to consumers. This is a commendable, professional approach to business.

Index